MANUAL FOR THE
PRACTICAL STOIC

MANUAL FOR THE PRACTICAL STOIC

A Stoic's Guide To Daily Living
Based On Stoic Ethics

KEVIN T. MALONE

ISBN-13: 979-8657148831
Library of Congress Control Number: 2018675309
Printed in the United States of America

Dedicated to my wonderful wife.

Contents

PREFACE

The intention of this book is to be used as a reference manual for the practice of Stoicism in modern day life. There is a need to organize and state plainly ways for Stoics to practice Stoicism; this should contain both traditional and modern techniques in an ordered fashion. Stoicism is a practical philosophy; the intention of it is to practice virtue and reason. As such, this book deals with and is concerned with the practice of ethics and virtue. Within the contents are four distinct sections: an Introduction, the Practice Section, the Maxim Section, and the Cognitive Bias Section. The Practice Section is a collection of ancient Stoic practices along with modern practices that a Stoic might have used in the past; this is further broken down into Foundational Practices, Important Practices, Good Practices, Intermediate Practices, and Advanced Practices. The Maxim Section of the book is broken down into four subsections: Maxims on Introspection, Maxims on Temperance, Maxims on Benevolence, and Maxims on Justice. The final section is a short list of common cognitive biases.

This book is meant to be mostly a reference guide. It is important to note that while some practices are seen as more necessary, this does not mean that other practices should be excluded as unimportant. The organization of this book is an attempt to organize practices by both their complexity and importance. Of course, there will inherently be some divisiveness over placement of some of the methods.

A few practices that are foundational are outlined in the Foundational Section and would be seen to an ancient Stoic to be almost necessary. These practices in this section are very important to living the philosophy of Stoicism. Methods noted in the Important Section are very important but not seen as foundational. These are meant for newcomers to Stoicism. Practices seen in the Good Practice Section are practices that enhance both foundational and important practices. Some of these are very important to Stoicism; however, they are not seen as necessary for someone new to Stoicism. The Intermediate Section includes good practices that may have been seen as important to ancient Stoics but are a bit more advanced. Finally, the Advanced Section is for more seasoned Stoics, as those practices may require a higher level of effort.

NOTES ON STOICISM

This book is not so much an introduction to Stoicism, but more so a guide on techniques that a modern Stoic might deem useful. It is highly recommended that one read the Enchiridion by Epictetus as an introductory text to get a feel of the basic principles of Stoicism. Epictetus was one of the great Stoics along with: Marcus Aurelius, Seneca the Younger, Gaius Musonius Rufus, Chrysippus, and Zeno of Citium. A more complete analysis of Stoicism and other Hellenistic philosophies could be obtained by reading Bertrand Russell's "The History of Western Philosophy".

Stoicism is a school of Hellenistic philosophy, which was founded in Athens, Greece, in the early 3rd century BCE by Zeno of Citium. Stoicism was originally known as Zenonism, after its founder; however, this name was changed later to Stoicism to reflect the Stoa Poikile or "painted porch." The Stoa was a row of columns engraved with mythic and historical battle scenes on the northern side of the Agora in Athens. This was a place where Stoic philosophy was often taught in ancient Greece.

It is important to note that our modern conceptions of philosophy are a bit different from the historical concepts of philosophy in ancient Greece. Philosophy was practiced then as a way to live one's life. The ancient Greeks defined philosophy as askêsis, an actual practice or exercise. They felt Stoicism was a philosophy that was designed to live in accordance with nature by becoming a rational, social, and virtuous member of humanity. Early Stoics did this by creating a number of tools to build resilience, mindfulness, understanding of self, and other ways to stay on the path of virtue. The study of Stoicism can be divided into three main categories: the study of ethics, the study of physical theory, and the study of logic.

The study of ethics is the most popularly discussed subject of Stoicism. Ethics concern the idea that one should first provide a specification of the telos, the goal or end of living. Cleanthes stated that the telos was "living in agreement with nature." The Stoics also founded the belief that virtue is the highest good, which was derived from formal logic. Virtue was defined by Stoics as: "Virtue consists in a will that is in agreement with Nature." Virtue was split into the four virtues of: temperance, courage, justice, and wisdom. Temperance is mentioned in many texts as being a very important as a means of overcoming potentially destructive emotions. Stoics would state that an unbiased and temperate person could allow for a person to come to understand universal reason – also defined as logos. In this the Stoics felt that not being in control of passions, or pathê – forms of emotional suffering such as: anger, fear or excessive joy – lead to a person being unreasonable. They again stated that to become free of suffering through apatheia – "without passions" – created a peace of mind that lead to a person being objective, clear in judgement, and with reason. Courage was important to the Stoics in that they felt it was fair and reasonable to speak out against injustice. To act against passions was considered an act of courage. Because humans are social creatures, the Stoics also felt that justice was essential for humanity. Wisdom in the form of logic and reason is what drives a rational and orderly world according to Epictetus. He further states that those who live in accordance to reason would feel the least amount of resistance to their lives because they would be living in accordance with nature.

Physical theory is a method of explaining the natural world and processes that work in the universe. Because science and technology were limited in this early time period, philosophy and logic were deemed suitable methods to describe and understand the world. One major idea of the Stoics' physical theory was the idea of pneuma, or divine essence that makes up all things—the matter of the universe. Another concept that was part of the Stoic physical theory is that of palingenesis, which is the concept of the destruction and creation of the universe in a never-ending cycle. Monism is the pantheistic idea the Stoics had that the universe is a rational and life-giving entity. In this, they explained that there is a logos that could explain everything such as natural events, human nature, and reason itself. Stoics also asserted that many things, including such abstract ideas as justice and wisdom, are corporeal. This idea of Materialism was further defined as meaning that all actions proceed by contact with bodies, communication from one body to another, with every causation being reduced to its efficient cause. Some ideas such as void and time, however, were recognized to be nonmaterial. Dynamism is a dualistic feature of Stoic physical theory holding that every existing thing is capable of acting or being acted upon. Although the Stoics considered the universe to have both active and passive qualities, it was likely that they saw the universe as a single gestalt universe. The Stoics also embraced a sort of determinism. They believed that even though humans had free will, there was an interconnected net of fate that was utterly and already determined by logos. While humans may make choices, ultimately their fate was already determined. The Stoics defined the soul as corporeal with its components being that of reason, logic, and the ruling principle. They thought that the soul was the spirit of the rational being. They stated that at birth a soul is a blank tablet because it is receptive to receive knowledge.

The study of logic was largely defined by Chrysippus. The entirety of what the Stoics called logic – logikê, or the knowledge of the functions of reason and logos – was very broad. Logic included the analysis of argument forms, rhetoric, grammar, concepts, propositions, perception, and thought. Logikê in this sense included not just our modern concept of logic, but also the philosophy of language and epistemology. An important part of logic is that it is based on the analysis of propositions, the smallest unit being the assertibles. These assertibles would have a value assigned to them, such that at any time they would be either true or false. In this way assertibles are very much like the modern-day idea of a proposition; however, the truth of the assertible also depended on when it were asserted. For example, the statement "it is day" is only true if stated during the day. These assertibles could then be built up through logic. This would be done through use of connective words such as: conjunctive (and), conditional (if), disjunctive (or), pseudoconditional (since), causal (because), and comparative (more/less likely it is …than …). These connective words would then make connections between assertibles to form a basis of logic. Chrysippus also set up a model to define the difference between necessary and possible truths. A necessary truth is an assertible that when it is true cannot become false, or it is prevented by external things from becoming false. By contrast, a non-necessary truth is an assertible that can become false and is not affected by external things from becoming false. A possible is an assertible that can become true and is not hindered by externals from becoming true, whereas an impossible is an assertible that cannot become true or can become true, but is hindered by externals from becoming true. In such, the Stoics were fond of formal logic and building on assertations. In particular – and an important part of Stoic training – was the subject of paradoxes. The logical training of Stoics included finding solutions to paradoxes. One example that Chrysippus was fond of is: "A man says he is lying. Is what he says true or false?" This paradox would challenge the principles of truth and falsehood for a Stoic. While the Stoics certainly engaged in abstract theory and the teaching of logic, logic was mostly meant to be applied to problems in daily life. Its aim was to bring about ethical reasoning, develop discourse, and ultimately lead to truth and understanding.

Stoicism exerted influence on many different areas in philosophy, religion, and society. Of particular interest, Stoicism had a significant influence on Christianity. Stoic writings, in particular those on the virtues, were seen as very favorable to early Christians. For instance, St. Thomas Aquinas wrote on the Stoics' definitions of virtue. In addition, Christian monks would often hand copy Stoic handbooks as pearls of wisdom. It has also been thought that Evagrius' notion of the seven deadly sins may have been derived from the Stoic ideas of freedom from passions. Natural law in Aquinas' ethical writings ("Summa Theologica") are strikingly similar to and may have been derived from Cicero ("de Legibus"). Later, during the Renaissance, there was a brief reemergence of Stoicism, most prominently through the work of Justus Lipsius. The reemergence of Stoicism in modern times has generally focused on the ways that Stoicism could be therapeutic. In fact, some Stoic practices have similarities with both the second and third waves of cognitive behavioral therapy (CBT). Nevertheless, it is important to note that while Stoicism has some very therapeutic practices, it was intended to be a way of living.

Algra, K. (2010). The Cambridge history of Hellenistic philosophy. Cambridge: Cambridge University Press.

Epictetus. (2004). Enchiridion. Mineola, NY: Dover Publ. Epictetus, & Dobbin, R. F. (2008).

Discourses and selected writings. London: Penguin. Hicks, Robert Drew (1911), "Stoics," in Chisholm, Hugh (ed.),

The Encyclopædia Britannica, 25, Cambridge University Press Gabbay, D. M., Woods, J., & Kanamori, A. (2004). Handbook of the history of logic. Amsterdam: Elsevier. Russell, B. (2015).

History of western philosophy. Routledge. Sellars, John (2006), Ancient Philosophies: Stoicism, Acumen Sorabji, R. (2010).

Emotion and peace of mind: From Stoic agitation to Christian temptation. Oxford: Oxford University Press.

Graphics

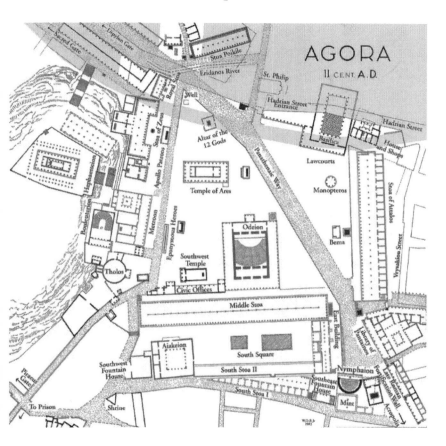

Credit: William Bell Dinsmoor Jr.

Timeline of Stoicism

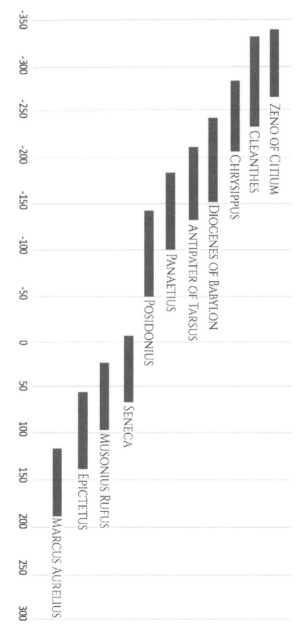

BEGINNER TO STOICISM

	MONDAY	TUESDAY	WEDNESDAY	THURSDAY	FRIDAY	SATURDAY	SUNDAY
MORNING	MAXIM / MEDITATION	MAXIM / MEDITATION	MAXIM / MEDITATION	MAXIM / MEDITATION	MAXIM / MEDITATION	MAXIM / MEDITATION	MAXIM / MEDITATION
MID-DAY		ONE GOOD PRACTICE		ONE GOOD PRACTICE		ONE GOOD PRACTICE	
EVENING	JOURNALING	JOURNALING	JOURNALING	JOURNALING	JOURNALING	JOURNALING	JOURNALING

INTERMEDIATE TO STOICISM

		MONDAY	TUESDAY	WEDNESDAY	THURSDAY	FRIDAY	SATURDAY	SUNDAY
MORNING		REFLECTION OF PASSAGE	REFLECTION OF PASSAGE	REFLECTION OF PASSAGE	REFLECTION OF PASSAGE	REFLECTION OF PASSAGE	REFLECTION OF PASSAGE	REFLECTION OF PASSAGE
		MEDITATION	MEDITATION	MEDITATION	MEDITATION	MEDITATION	MEDITATION	MEDITATION
MID-DAY		ONE GOOD PRACTICE	ONE IMPORTANT PRACTICE	ONE GOOD PRACTICE	ONE IMPORTANT PRACTICE	ONE GOOD PRACTICE	ONE IMPORTANT PRACTICE	
EVENING		JOURNALING	JOURNALING	JOURNALING	JOURNALING	VOLUNTARY DISCOMFORT	JOURNALING VIEW FROM ABOVE	JOURNALING
						JOURNALING		

VALUES UP TO US	GOOD THINGS (ta agatha, bona)	BAD THINGS (ta kaka, mala)
Character Traits	Virtues (hai aretai virtutes) 1. Wisdom (sophia, sapientia) 2. Justice (dikaiosune) 3. Bravery (andreia) 4. Temperance (sophrosune) 5. Generosity	Vices (hai kakiai) 1. Folly (or ignorance) 2. Injustice (adikia) 3. Cowardice 4. Intemperance (akolasia) 5. Ungenerosity
Acts	Virtuous Acts 1. Wise acts 2. Just acts 3. Brave acts 4. Temperate acts 5. Generous acts	Vicious Acts 1. Foolish acts 2. Unjust acts 3. Cowardly acts 4. Intemperate acts 5. Ungenerous acts
Feelings	Good Feelings (hai eupatheiai) 1. Wish (boulesis) 2. Caution (eulabeia) 3. Joy (chara)	Passions or Violent Feelings (pathe) 1. Lust (epithumia, libido) 2. Fear (phobos) 3. Delight (hedone, laeticia) 4. Distress (lupe, aegritudo)

Preferred Things (*ta proegmena*)	**Rejected Things** (*t' apoproegmena*)
1. Survival or mere life	1. Death
2. Physical beauty	2. Ugliness
3. Health	3. Illness
4. Popularity	4. Unpopularity
5. "Good" reputation	5. "Bad" reputation
6. Wealth	6. Poverty
7. Technical ability	7. Lack of technical ability

Foundational Practices

Stoic Affirmation / Maxims

Practice:

· Read a maxim out loud and try to reflect and ask how it can apply to one's life.

Intent:

· Internalize knowledge but ultimately spark action and facilitate wiser decisions.
· Following your principles.
· Develop / strengthen the neural pathways for the Stoic mindset / perspective / identity.

Effect:

· Allow for the possibility to get a visceral feeling of having a Stoic mindset.

Example:

You decide you would like to better embody Stoic practices. To achieve this, you decide that reading a daily maxim is a good way to remind oneself of Stoic concepts. It was decided to be wise to start today because that is what is within your control. You read your first maxim: "I do not and cannot control the events outside me. I can only control how I respond to them." You then ask yourself "how this can apply to me and my life today?"

Sources:

"Don't just say you have read books. Show that through them you have learned to think better, to be a more discriminating and reflective person. Books are the training weights of the mind. They are very helpful, but it would be a bad mistake to suppose that one has made progress simply by having internalized their contents."

- Epictetus

"A man ought to know that it is not easy for him to have an opinion (or fixed principle), if he does not daily say the same things, and hear the same things, and at the same time apply them to life." -Epictetus

Epictetus. (2004). *Enchiridion*. Mineola, NY: Dover Publ.

Epictetus, & Lebell, S. (1995). The art of living: The classical manual on virtue, happiness, and effectiveness. New York: HarperOne.

Reflections on Stoic Passages

<u>Practice</u>:

· Reading a passage from a Stoic work with reflection of it.

<u>Effect</u>:

· Allow the possibility of a visceral Stoic mindset.

<u>Long term Intent</u>:

· Develop / strengthen the neural pathways for the Stoic mindset, perspective, and identity.

<u>Example</u>:

Read a passage every morning from Enchiridion or Letters from a Stoic. You should reflect on the passage for a few minutes. Reflection is an important part of this. It might be helpful to write down your thoughts on the passage and how it affects you. Early on it is useful to focus on just a few Stoic authors.

<u>Sources</u>:

"You must linger among a limited number of master thinkers, and digest their works, if you would derive ideas which shall win firm hold in your mind. Nothing hinders a cure so much as frequent change of medicine". – Seneca

"Each day, acquire something that will fortify you against poverty, against death, indeed against other misfortunes as well; and after you have run over many thoughts, select one to be thoroughly digested that day." - Seneca

"What's the point of having countless books and libraries, whose titles could hardly be read through in a lifetime. The learner is not taught, but burdened by the sheer volume, and it's better to plant the seeds of a few authors than to be scattered about by many" - Seneca

"We should not use philosophy like a herbal remedy, to be discarded when we're through. Rather, we must allow philosophy to remain with us, continually guarding our judgements throughout life, forming part of our daily regimen, like eating a nutritious diet or taking physical exercise." - Musonius Rufus

"Therefore practicing each virtue always must follow learning the lessons appropriate to it, or it is pointless for us to learn about it. The person who claims to be studying philosophy must practice it even more diligently than the person who aspires to the art of medicine or some similar skill, inasmuch as philosophy is more important and harder to grasp than any other pursuit." - Musonius Rufus

Rufus, C. M., Irvine, W. B., & King, C. A. (2011). Musonius Rufus: Lectures & sayings. Lexington, KY: Createspace.

Seneca, L. A., & Campbell, R. (2014). Letters from a Stoic – Epistulae morales ad Lucilium. London: Penguin Classics, an imprint of Penguin Books.

Good Luck or Bad Luck

Practice:

· Remind yourself of the moral of the story from the "Chinese Farmer" story: *"Maybe it's good luck, maybe it's bad luck. We'll see"* or *"You never know what will be the consequence of the misfortune; or, you never know what will be the consequences of good fortune."*

Effect:

· Remember the fact you can't predict the future or the course of things of an alternative reality in order to absolutely classify anything under either good or bad.

Intent:

· Remind and develop the habit of humility and the wisdom of "withholding from judgements."

Example:

"Once upon a time there was a Chinese farmer whose horse ran away. That evening, all of his neighbors came around to commiserate. They said, 'We are so sorry to hear your horse has run away. This is most unfortunate.' The farmer said, 'Maybe.' The next day the horse came back bringing seven wild horses with it, and in the evening everybody came back and said, 'Oh, isn't that lucky. What a great turn of events. You now have eight horses!' The farmer again said, 'Maybe.' The following day his son tried to break one of the horses, and while riding it, he was thrown and broke his leg. The neighbors then said, 'Oh dear, that's too bad,' and the farmer responded, 'Maybe.' The next day the conscription officers came around to conscript people into the army, and they rejected his son because he had a broken leg. Again all the neighbors came around and said, 'Isn't that great!' Again, he said, 'Maybe.'"
- Alan Watts

Next time you forget your wallet and you get upset, say "Maybe it's bad luck, or maybe it's good luck."

Sources:

The whole process of nature is an integrated process of immense complexity, and it's really impossible to tell whether anything that happens in it is good or bad —

because you never know what will be the consequence of the misfortune; or, you never know what will be the consequences of good fortune. You never know what will be the consequence of the misfortune; or, you never know what will be the consequences of good fortune.
- Alan Watts

"I was once a fortunate man but at some point fortune abandoned me. But true good fortune is what you make for yourself. Good fortune: good character, good intentions, and good actions. Be a good person. "
- Marcus Aurelius

"Whatever happens to you has been waiting to happen since the beginning of time. The twining strands of fate wove both of them together."
- Marcus Aurelius

"When Zeno received news of a shipwreck and heard that all his luggage had been sunk he said, "Fortune bids me to be a less encumbered philosopher." -Seneca

"What fortune has made yours is not your own." - Seneca

Aurelius, M., & Long, G. (2018). The meditations. Mineola, New York.: Dover Publications.

Seneca, L. A., & Campbell, R. (2014). *Letters from a Stoic - Epistulae morales ad Lucilium.* London: Penguin Classics, an imprint of Penguin Books.

Watts, A. (2011). *Eastern wisdom, modern life: Collected talks, 1960-1969.* New World Library.

Journaling

Practice:

· Journaling should be a practice done at night with purpose. This would involve reflecting on the finished day and reviewing one's actions.

Intent:

· Self mastery in one's self.

· Improved insight in the future.

· Gain in insight and wisdom

Effect:

· Gain in insight, wisdom, and reflection into one's own actions.

· To put the day to a conclusion.

<u>Example:</u>

Did I act according to my principles today? Have I treated the people with whom I interacted with in a friendly and considerate manner? What vices did I fight? What virtue have I practiced? Have I made myself a better person today by means of virtues? At the end of the journal, you should remind yourself that this day has finished and there is nothing you can now do to change it. Accept your day as finished and that it is neither "good" or "bad."

<u>Sources:</u>

"Never allow sleep to close your eyelids, after you went to bed, until you have examined all your actions of the day by your reason. In what have I done wrong? What have I done? What have I omitted that I ought to have done? If in this examination you find that you have done wrong, reprove yourself severely for it; And if you have done any good, rejoice. Practice thoroughly all these things; meditate on them well; you ought to love them with all your heart. It is those that will put you in the way of divine virtue."
- The Golden Verses of Pythagoras

"When the light has been removed and my wife has fallen silent, aware of this habit that's now mine, I examine my entire day and go back over what I've done and said, hiding nothing from myself, passing nothing by." - Seneca

D'Olivet, A. F., Pythagoras, & Redfield, N. L. (1983). The Golden verses of Pythagoras. New York: Concord Grove Press.

Seneca, L. A., & Campbell, R. (2014). Letters from a Stoic - Epistulae morales ad Lucilium. London: Penguin Classics, an imprint of Penguin Books.

Mindfulness Meditation

Practice:

· To concentrate on the present moment and not becoming concerned with the past or future.

Intent:

· The intent of this practice should be to center your mind on the present moment, and to reduce our bias placed on events and objects.

Effect:

· Enhances attention to the present moment.
· Become present in the moment.
· May help to reduce one's perception of stress.
· May help to improve one's cognition.

Example:

Mindfulness meditation is split into two parts nonjudgement and awareness. Nonjudgement refers to the ability to experience the sensation or thought without making judgements and seeing the world without judgements and biases. Awareness concerns our ability to perceive the "here and now." Holding an object such as a heavy stone, and drawing your attention to the stone, may be helpful to increase focus.

Find a quiet place to sit for a few minutes. Ask yourself as you start why you are meditating? Set a timer and make sure you commit to meditation. First bring your attention to your breath. Notice when your breathing feels the strongest. When you get distracted, notice that you are distracted, and return your attention to the breath. This can be done by saying "distraction" in your head. Continue breathing and returning yourself back to breathing whenever you become distracted. When the time is up, take a few deep breaths and open your eyes. Remember to immediately reflect on the meditation.

Sources:

"Concentrate every minute like a Roman–like a man–on doing what's in front of you with precise and genuine seriousness, tenderly, willingly, with justice. And on freeing yourself from all other distractions." -Marcus Aurelius

"We suffer more often in imagination than in reality." - Marcus Aurelius

"Today I escaped anxiety. Or no, I discarded it, because it was within me, in my own perceptions - not outside." - Marcus Aurelius

Abbasi, Jennifer. "Meditation App Improves Attention in Young Adults." Jama, vol. 322, no. 6, 2019, p. 495., doi:10.1001/jama.2019.11649.

Aurelius, M., & Long, G. (2018). The meditations. Mineola, New York.: Dover Publications.

Hoge, Elizabeth A., et al. "Randomized Controlled Trial of Mindfulness Meditation for Generalized Anxiety Disorder." The Journal of Clinical Psychiatry, vol. 74, no. 08, 2013, pp. 786–792., doi:10.4088/jcp.12m08083.

McGreevey, Sue. "'Turn down the Volume'." Harvard Gazette, Harvard Gazette, 14 June 2019,

Zeidan, Fadel, et al. "Mindfulness Meditation Improves Cognition: Evidence of Brief Mental Training." Consciousness and Cognition, vol. 19, no. 2, 2010, pp. 597–605., doi:10.1016/j.concog.2010.03.014.

Important Practices

Negative Visualization

Practice:

· Imagine the worst-case scenario in certain situations with as visceral of imagination as possible.

Intent:

· Realize and practice one's skill to self-reliantly respond and deal with a future similar situation.
· Realize the burden of attachments.

Effect:

· Attain the ability to respond effectively to adverse situations.
· Release one's self of the attachment.

Examples:

Things one might want to apply to negative visualization: mortality, health, loss of family members, loss of possessions, becoming imprisoned/slave, loss of senses or limbs, and social shaming.

Imagine coming home to where you live, and everything is missing. There is only a floor and walls left. Imagine how you would feel, how your chest would feel heavy and hurt from being so upset. Then think how it could be worse. What might happen? Are there any opportunities that can be gained from losing your possessions? Now open your eyes and see that everything is still present.

The practice of *memento mori* is to remind ourselves that we are mortal and are going to die. One should not think passively, but to actively visualize the slow process of dying. Thinking about death puts your own life into perspective. Life is always losing time. This process should incite gratitude and appreciation for your life.

Another expression is *premeditatio malorum,* this is the acknowledgement of the evils and troubles that may happen to us in the future. Premeditatio malorum is imagining things that may go wrong or be taken from us. Bad things will happen to you in your life. You should prepare yourself for difficulties that might happen so that when they do - we can handle them with resilience. When things are unexpected, they have a worse impact, this is why we should prepare for the unexpected in advance.

Sources:
"Never say of anything, 'I have lost it', but 'I have returned

it.' Is your child dead? It is returned. Is your wife dead? She is returned. Is your estate taken away? Well, and is not that likewise returned? 'But he who took it away is a bad man.' What difference is it to you who the giver assigns to take it back? While he gives it to you to possess, take care of it; but don't view it as your own, just as travelers view a hotel." - Epictetus

"Let us prepare our minds as if we'd come to the very end of life. Let us postpone nothing. Let us balance life's books each day... The one who puts the finishing touches on their life each day is never short of time." - Seneca

Epictetus. (2004). Enchiridion. Mineola, NY: Dover Publ.

Seneca, L. A., & Campbell, R. (2014). Letters from a Stoic – Epistulae morales ad Lucilium. London: Penguin Classics

Ready Your Tools

Practice:

· One should have a list of available tools that might help them in a difficult situation. Remember that having a list of tools should never be used as an excuse to not use them. You can spend so much time getting ready to live that you never get around to living.

Intent:

· Practice virtue with reason.

Effect:

· A ready list of tools to use when the situation arises.
· Knowledge of knowing the right tools when faced with a challenge.

Example:

Have memorized a few helpful maxims regarding your philosophy to recite throughout the day. Quotes, maxims, the basics of your belief system - whatever it takes to bring you back to the center of Stoicism. Keep copies of Meditations, The Enchiridion at hand. Know some Stoic practices to use in choice situations.

Sources:

"As physicians have always their instruments and knives ready for cases that suddenly require their skill, so do you have principles ready for the understanding of things divine and human, and for doing everything, even the smallest, with a recollection of the bond that unites the divine and human to each other." - Marcus Aurelius

"Every habit and faculty is formed or strengthened by the corresponding act – walking makes you walk better, running makes you a better runner. If you want to be literate, read, if you want to be a painter, paint…So if you like doing something, do it regularly; if you don't like doing something, make a habit of doing something different." - Epictetus

Aurelius, M., & Long, G. (2018). The meditations. Mineola, New York.: Dover Publications.

Epictetus. (2004). Enchiridion. Mineola, NY: Dover Publ.

Grid of Control

Practice:

· When dealing with a problem, create a list of things that are in one's control and things that are out of one's control. Then ask yourself how you can handle the things that are in your control.

Intent:

· Recognize one's locus of control and to distinguish what is in and not in one's control.

Effect:

· Recognize the things that are in one's control and not in one's control.

· Distinguish priorities that one can control and work on.

Example:

Your flight is delayed due to poor weather conditions. You could become angry and get mad at the situation or you can physically list things that are in and not in your control.

You decide that you list things that are in and not in your control in order to be productive. This way you might distinguish priorities that you can work on or things that might not be in your control.

Not in your control:	In your control:
Weather	Your perceptions of the delayed flight
Lost time	Your emotions towards the event
	How you can spend your time

After you finish making your list you draw a clearer understanding of what you can do with your time. Instead of focusing on the weather and getting mad at the time you have lost, you can focus on living in virtue and take this as a challenge. You take out your phone and spend your time reading, sending emails, and doing other productive things.

(next page)

Is there a problem in your life?

Yes

No

Is it within your control?

Yes

No

Then there is no cause for concern.

Sources:

"Of all existing things some are in our power, and others are not in our power. In our power are thought, impulse, will to get and will to avoid, and, in a word, everything which is our own doing. Things not in our power include the body, property, reputation, office, and, in a word, everything which is not our own doing. Things in our power are by nature free, unhindered, untrammelled; things not in our power are weak, servile, subject to hindrance, dependent on others. Remember then that if you imagine that what is naturally slavish is free, and what is naturally another's is your own, you will be hampered, you will mourn, you will be put to confusion, you will blame gods and men; but if you think that only your own belongs to you, and that what is another's is indeed another's, no one will ever put compulsion or hindrance on you, you will blame none, you will accuse none, you will do nothing against your will, no one will harm you, you will have no enemy, for no harm can touch you." - Epictetus

Epictetus. (2004). Enchiridion. Mineola, NY: Dover Publ.

Amor Fati

Practice:

· Accept fate through: acceptance of reality for what it is, nonjudgement of a situation, unattachment from externals.

Intent:

· Embracing fate as out of one's control.
· Release the self from worry.

Effect:

· Learn to focus on what is able to be controlled.
· Learn that fate is out of their control.

Example:

You may work hard at your job at work, however, lose your job due to economic difficulties. You recognize that to get angry at fate for this situation would be unproductive. Instead you might accept fate for what it is. You would not say that "this is horrible, I lost my job" instead might say "I lost my job and nothing more." You would tell yourself that fate is not within my control, so to hate fate would be to fight with reality.

Sources:

"What is quite unlooked for is more crushing in its effect, and unexpectedness adds to the weight of a disaster. This is a reason for ensuring that nothing ever takes us by surprise. We should project our thoughts ahead of us at every turn and have in mind every possible eventuality instead of only the usual course of events... Rehearse them in your mind: exile, torture, war, shipwreck. All the terms of our human lot should be before our eyes."
- Seneca

"Fate leads the willing and drags along the reluctant."
– Seneca

"They too [Zeno and Chrysippus] affirmed that everything is fated, with the following model: When a dog is tied to a cart, if it wants to follow it is pulled and follows, making its spontaneous act coincide with necessity, but if it does not want to follow it will be compelled in any case. So it is with men too: even if they do not want to, they will be compelled in any case to follow what is destined."

Long, A. A., & Sedley, D. N. (1987). The Hellenistic philosophers. Cambridge: Cambridge University Press.

Seneca, L. A., & Campbell, R. (2014). *Letters from a Stoic - Epistulae morales ad Lucilium*. London: Penguin Classics

The View from Above

Practice:

· This is a practice based in visualization to reframe a situation. It is a guided visualization which is aimed at instilling a sense of the 'bigger picture', and of understanding your role in the wider world.

· In the view from above, you literally visualize yourself and your situation from an increasingly larger scope with as much detail as you can imagine.

Intent:

· Intent of this exercise is to reframe your situation.

· Contextualize one's self within the scope of the universe.

Effect:

· *Transframing.* Reframes your world and self in such a way that it can make you more insightful, equanimous, self aware, and responsible.

· Gain a better insight to the scale of your problems.

Example:

Your girlfriend/boyfriend has recently left you. You feel as though you want to try a "view from above" in order to alleviate your suffering. You decide to lay in your bed and close your eyes to get comfortable. You imagine yourself as clearly as you can in your bed as you are currently as though you were looking at yourself from across the room. You then "float up" above your house and imagine, as clearly as you can your neighborhood. You then go higher and imagine your city, your state, and your country. You see the vastness of the country with its coast, large fields, and mountains, you go out further and see the entirety of the world. With the enormous size of the world you see all the problems in the poor countries, suffering, and how many people and problems there are all over the world. You decide to go out further, past Mars, past Jupiter, and out at the end of the solar system. You find it difficult to grasp the vastness of the solar system, but you decide to look out into the universe, and see all the galaxies, all of the, black holes, and the uncountable planets. You suddenly remember that you did this to reframe your situation, and right now it doesn't seem quite as bad anymore.

Sources:

"You can rid yourself of many useless things among those that disturb you, for they lie entirely in your imagination; and you will then gain for yourself ample space by comprehending the whole universe in your mind, and by contemplating the eternity of time, and observing the rapid change of every part of everything, how short is the time from birth to dissolution, and the illimitable time before birth as well as the equally boundless time after dissolution." - Marcus Aurelius

"Plato has a fine saying, that he who would discourse of man should survey, as from some high watchtower, the things of earth." - Marcus Aurelius

Aurelius, M., & Long, G. (2018). The meditations. Mineola, New York.: Dover Publications.

Everything is Borrowed from Fortune

Practice:

· Remind oneself that everything is borrowed and can be taken away at any moment.

Effect:

· Visceral reminder of the possibility of losing your possessions.
· Greater appreciation for things in one's life.

Intent:

· Restructuring of your identity such that you're emotionally detached from externals.

Example:

When enjoying an externals or the company of a friend you might remind yourself that these things may be temporary and can be lost at any moment. You might say "I do not own these things, but I only borrow them from fortune". This might make you become more attentive with your friend or possessions.

Sources:

"We have no grounds for self-admiration, as though we were surrounded by our own possessions; they have been loaned to us. We may use and enjoy them, but the one who allotted his gift decides how long we are to be tenants; our duty is to keep ready the gifts we have been given for an indefinite time and to return them when called upon, making no complaint: it is a sorry debtor who abuses his creditor." - Seneca

"What fortune has made yours is not your own." - Seneca

"Whatever happens to you has been waiting to happen since the beginning of time. The twining strands of fate wove both of them together." - Marcus Aurelius

"Never say of anything, 'I have lost it;' but, 'I have restored it.' Has your child died? It is restored. Has your wife died? She is restored. Has your estate been taken away? That likewise is restored. 'But it was a bad man who took it.' What is it to you by whose hands he who gave it has demanded it again? While he permits you to possess it, hold it as something not your won; as do travelers at an inn." -Epictetus

"The life which is implicated with fortune (depends on fortune) is like a winter torrent: for it is turbulent, and full of mud, and difficult to cross, and tyrannical, and noisy, and of short duration." -Epictetus

Aurelius, M., & Long, G. (2018). The meditations. Mineola, New York.: Dover Publications.

Epictetus. (2004). Enchiridion. Mineola, NY: Dover Publ.

Seneca, L. A., & Campbell, R. (2014). Letters from a Stoic Epistulae morales ad Lucilium. London: Penguin Classics, an imprint of Penguin Books.

Good Practices

Centering Reminder

Practice:

· Wear something that can remind oneself of something meaningful in the day.

Intent:

· Re-center one's self to a set meaning.

Effect:

· Reminder to keep attention to virtues
· Incidental reminder throughout the day.

Example:

Wrap a bit of string around your wrist. Associate it with a meaning or a maxim such as one's own mortality "memento mori." Do this by saying "When I see this string randomly in the day, I will remember my own mortality." Throughout the day when the string is recognized it will remind you of why you placed it there. "I wrapped this string on my left wrist, so that when I see it I am reminded that I can die at any moment."

The application of an annoyance such as an itchy necklace, or heavy weight in a pocket may enhance this method.

This reminder might be alternated often so that the user will not become accustomed to it.

Add a Reserve Clause

Other names: hupexhairesis

Practice:

· Add a reserve clause to one's actions or statements such as "if nothing prevents me."

Intent:

· Acceptance that some things are not in one's control.

Effect:

· Reminder of the uncertainty of things.
· Statement of a way to succeed and simultaneously recognize fate.
· Know and accept that the ultimate outcome is beyond your direct control.

Example:

You are getting ready to take an exam. You are feeling nervous. You decide to use the reserve clause technique to help yourself in this situation. You say: "I will do my best if nothing prevents me." This reminds you of what is in your control--your actions--and what is not in your control--your fate.

Sources:

"I will sail across the ocean, if nothing prevents me." - Seneca

"In short, the wise man looks to the purpose of all actions, not their consequences; beginnings are in our power, but Fortune judges the outcome, and I do not grant her a verdict upon me."
-Seneca

"Everything suits me that suits your designs, O my universe. Nothing is too early or too late for me that is in your own good time." - Marcus Aurelius

"The non-destruction of one's coat is not fated simply, but co-fated with its being taken care of, and someone's being saved from his enemies is co-fated with his fleeing those enemies; and having children is co-fated with being willing to lie with a woman. ... For many things cannot occur without our being willing and indeed contributing a most strenuous eagerness and zeal for these things, since, he says, it was fated for these things to occur in conjunction with this personal effort. ... But it will be in our power with what is in our power being included in fate."

- Chrysippus

Aurelius, M., & Long, G. (2018). *The meditations*. Mineola, New York.: Dover Publications.

Inwood, B. (2006). Hellenistic philosophy: Introductory readings. Indianapolis: Hackett Publ.

Seneca, L. A., & Campbell, R. (2014). Letters from a Stoic Epistulae morales ad Lucilium. London: Penguin Classics, an imprint of Penguin Books.

Reflection on Self

Practice:

· In response to others: When there is an accusation or action taken against one, it may be prudent to reflect on the self before taking judgement.

Intent:

· Reflection and understanding of oneself.
· Understanding of our motivations.
· Understanding of others' motivations.

Effect:

· Empathize and reframe judgements and actions of others.
· Evaluation and process what our experiences.

Example:

Ask yourself were you in the person's shoes would you have acted the same or said the same thing. When the person feels wronged, ask yourself exactly what it is that you might have done; This may put the other person's situation into perspective and allow you to empathize with them.

Sources:

"When a man has done you wrong, immediately consider with what opinion about good
or evil he has done wrong. For when you have seen this, you will pity him, and will neither wonder nor be angry. For either you yourself think the same thing to be good that he does or another thing of the same kind. It is your duty then to pardon him. But if you do not think such things to be good or evil, you will more readily be well disposed to him who is in error." - Marcus Aurelius

"To accuse others for one's own misfortune is a sign of want of education. To accuse oneself shows that one's education has begun. To accuse neither oneself nor others shows that one's education is complete." - Epictetus

"Do not give judgement in one court (of justice) before you yourself fail (stumble) least in your life." - Epictetus

"When you're about to embark on any action, remind yourself what kind of action it is. If you're going out to take a bath, set before your mind the things that happen at the baths, that people splash you, that people knock up against you, that people steal from you. And you'll thus undertake the action in a surer manner if you say to yourself at the outset, 'I want to take a bath and ensure at the same time that my choice remains in harmony with nature.'" - Epictetus

"It is the act of an ill-instructed man to blame others for his own bad condition; it is the act of one who has begun to be instructed, to lay the blame on himself; and of one whose instruction is completed, neither to blame another, nor himself." -Epictetus

"The unexamined life is not worth living." - Socrates

Aurelius, M., & Long, G. (2018). The meditations. Mineola, New York.: Dover Publications.

Epictetus. (2004). Enchiridion. Mineola, NY: Dover Publ.

Jowett, B. (2012). The Republic by Plato. Luton: AUK Classics.

Daily Virtue Focus

Practice:

· When you wake up, set your day to have a focus on one virtue for the day.

Intent:

· Better practice of all virtues.

Effect:

· Clear focus on a specific virtue.
· Better understanding in a specific virtue.

Example:

You wake up in the morning and decide to tell yourself that your focus is on temperance today. You will still practice all virtues, however for today you will intensely focus on temperance. You state: "I will practice temperance today." Throughout the day, you focus on temperance, when you decide to eat, you eat in moderation. When you decide to speak to others, you decide not to be loose with words. Tomorrow you might decide to focus on courage in action and in words.

The virtues:

Wisdom - knowing what is good and bad.

Justice - moral wisdom, impartiality.

Temperance - moderation, and self-control.

Courage - bravery, grit, resilience.

<u>Sources</u>:

"Virtues, as we call them, are often a series of acts and interest which chance, or our own diligence, has arranged."
- La Rochefoucauld

"So every occupation and manner of life, if attended by virtue, is untroubled and delightful, while, on the other hand, any admixture of vice renders those things which to others seem splendid, precious, in imposing, only troublesome, sickening, and unwelcome to their possessors." - Plutarch

Rochefoucauld, F. L., & Stack, E. M. (2005). *La Rochefoucauld maxims: A new English translation.* Vantage Press.

Plutarch, & Babbit, F. C. (1957). Plutarch Moralia. London: Heinemann.

Review the Company You Keep

Practice:

· A deliberate review of one's own company.

Intent:

· Surrounding oneself with people who improve one's life.

Effect:

· Realization of persons who are important in one's life.
· Realization of persons who should not be present in one's life.

Example:

You might want to surround yourself with people who are rational, who challenge themselves and others, who believe things different (with good reason), and people who might make you wiser for having spent time with them. Conversely, you might want to avoid people who bring out your worst. People who drag you back into bad habits, and who appeal to your baser instincts. Take a deliberate review of who you spend your company with and ask why they are important, or if they bring you down.

Sources:

"Avoid fraternizing with non-philosophers. If you must, though, be careful not to sink to their level; because, you know, if a companion is dirty, his friends cannot help but get a little dirty too, no matter how clean they started out."
- Epictetus

"The key is to keep company only with people who uplift you, whose presence calls forth your best." - Epictetus

"Instead of a herd of oxen, endeavor to assemble herds of friends in your house." -Epictetus

"We ought to avoid the friendship of the bad and the enmity of the good." - Epictetus

"Associate with people who are likely to improve you."
- Seneca

"Give a flatterer absurd advice and speak impertinently of his undertaking and he will agree with your disagreeable counsel." - Plutarch

"I don't need a friend who changes when I change and who nods when I nod; my shadow does that much better."
- Plutarch

Epictetus. (2004). Enchiridion. Mineola, NY: Dover Publ.

Plutarch, & Babbit, F. C. (1957). Plutarch Moralia. London: Heinemann.

Seneca, L. A., & Campbell, R. (2014). *Letters from a Stoic - Epistulae morales ad Lucilium.* London: Penguin Classics, an imprint of Penguin Books.

Voluntary Discomfort

Practice:

· This is a practice of inducing a physical stress in order to become comfortable with discomfort. · It allows one to experience gratitude and prepares one for future difficulties that may occur.

Intent:

· Tranquility of the mind.

· Greater appreciation.

· Stronger general willpower.

· Become comfortable with discomfort.

Effect:

· Decrease the attachments for material possessions.

· Decrease the appetite for sensual pleasures.

· Increase the appreciation for what one already has.

· Guard oneself against future misfortunes.

· Fasting may help with health and the immunity system.

· Cold showers may help with health.

Example:

There is a large number of ways to practice voluntary discomfort. You might try fasting for a period of time such as skipping a few meals. You also might think about taking cold showers to exert your will. Walking underdressed or dressed uncomfortably in public might cause physical discomfort or test your feelings of shame. Temporary poverty, treating yourself as if you were poor or even sleeping on the floor would be advocated by the Stoics.

Sources:

"The man who eats more than he ought does wrong, and the man who eats in undue haste no less, and also the man who wallows in the pickles and sauces, and the man who prefers the sweeter foods to the more healthful ones, and the man who does not serve food of the same kind or amount to his guests as to himself." -Musonius Rufus

"We will train both soul and body when we accustom ourselves to cold, heat, thirst, hunger, scarcity of food, hardness of bed, abstaining from pleasures, and enduring pains." - Musonius Rufus

"Check (punish) your passions, that you may not be punished by them." -Epictetus

"Those who are well constituted in the body endure both heat and cold: and so those who are well constituted in the soul endure both anger and grief and excessive joy and the other affects." -Epictetus

Aly, Salah Mesalhy. "Role of intermittent fasting on improving health and reducing diseases." *International journal of health sciences* vol. 8,3 (2014): V-VI. doi:10.12816/0023985

Buijze, Geert A et al. "The Effect of Cold Showering on Health and Work: A Randomized Controlled Trial." *PloS one* vol. 11,9 e0161749. 15 Sep. 2016, doi:10.1371/journal.pone.0161749

Epictetus. (2004). Enchiridion. Mineola, NY: Dover Publ.

Janský, L et al. "Immune system of cold-exposed and cold-adapted humans." *European journal of applied physiology and occupational physiology* vol. 72,5-6 (1996): 445-50. doi:10.1007/BF00242274

Rufus, C. M., Irvine, W. B., & King, C. A. (2011). Musonius Rufus: Lectures & sayings. Lexington, KY: Createspace.

Exercise

Practice:

· One should practice physical training to practice virtue.

Intent:

· Cultivation of a healthy mind and body.

Effect:

· Physical wellbeing.

· Mental clarity and increased cognition.

· Bodies are kept ready in good working condition.

Example:

Exercise should be about self-mastery and the cultivation of a healthy mind and body. One might participate in a martial art, sports, yoga, weightlifting or some sort of recurring physical activity. The cultivation of a working and able body prepares one for future struggles; it can help us exert fortitude and temperance.

Sources:

"It is a disgrace to grow old through sheer carelessness before seeing what manner of man you may become by developing your bodily strength and beauty to their highest limit." -Socrates

"To progress again, man must remake himself. And he cannot remake himself without suffering. For he is both the marble and the sculptor. In order to uncover his true visage he must shatter his own substance with heavy blows of his hammer." - Alexis Carrel

"Since a human being happens to be neither soul alone nor body alone, but a composite of these two things, someone in training must pay attention to both. He should, rightly pay more attention to the better part, namely the soul, but he should also take care of the other parts, or part of him will become defective. The philosopher's body also must be well prepared for work because often virtues use it as a necessary tool for the activities of life. Fitness routine can teach us virtuous life skills such as perseverance, self-improvement, discipline, overcoming challenges, and building self-confidence." - Musonius Rufus

Carrel, A. (2016). Man the unknown. Wilco Publishing House.

Mandolesi, Laura et al. "Effects of Physical Exercise on Cognitive Functioning and Wellbeing: Biological and Psychological Benefits." Frontiers in psychology vol. 9 509. 27 Apr. 2018, doi:10.3389/fpsyg.2018.00509

Warburton, Darren E R et al. "Health benefits of physical activity: the evidence." CMAJ : Canadian Medical Association journal = journal de l'Association medicale canadienne vol. 174,6 (2006): 801-9. doi:10.1503/cmaj.051351

Xenophon, & Marshall, J. (1890). Xenophon Memorabilia. Oxford: At the Clarendon Press.

Philanthropy

Practice:

· Promoting the welfare of others, expressed by the generous donation of money, time, or services for good causes. Human beings ought to develop their natural concern for others in a way that is congruent with the exercise of the virtue of justice.

Intent:

· To help promote welfare to others.
· Cause positive change in the world.
· To restrict one's self from overindulgence.

Effect:

· Create positive changes in world.
· Better understanding of justice.

Example:

Donating one's time to help at a homeless shelter, giving money -with purpose- to a good cause, and donating excess possessions. One good practice is to reduce one's own possessions, through donations, to practice minimalism while helping others.

Sources:

"Men exist for the sake of one another. Teach them then or bear with them." -Marcus Aurelius

Aurelius, M., & Long, G. (2018). The meditations. Mineola, New York.: Dover Publications.

Enacted Imagined Scenarios

Practice:

· Intended to be a group activity. Theatrical role play where people take on roles with a partner and imagine a fictitious, but realistic scenario that is realistic. This is done so that it could challenge one's Stoic views and techniques. The partner should challenge you, even harshly during the scenario.

Intent:

· To practice situations that may occur in daily life with a partner to work out challenges before they occur.

· Obtain a better understanding of how to act in certain situations.

Effect:

· Take on issues in a controlled environment so that in the future when running into a similar problem you may handle it in a preferred manner.

· To discuss between partners whether an action would be appropriate.

Example:

You and your friend are walking to the grocery store. The store is four miles away. You arrive at the store and go and grab all of your groceries. You go to pay and you realize you have forgotten your wallet at home. How do you feel? What are your thoughts on it? Your friend then gets mad at you and calls you an idiot, how do you respond? Is it reasonable to be angry in this situation?

Minimalism

Other names: Living simply

Practice:

· Simplify things in life. Removal of time wasters and unnecessary things.

Intent:

· To gain a better appreciation of material things.
· Preserve energy from unnecessary distractions.

Effect:

· Less distractions present.
· Decreased attachments from externals.
· To simplify things in one's life.

Example:

Take several days in the year to set aside time to remove unnecessary things from your life that you can do without. This can be the removal of physical objects, or things that might be time wasters. One should not make their goal for the obtainment of *arete'* - or fulfillment through excellence of character.

You might review and reflect on what they spend time on with the intent to remove for example three items today from your life; is there something you might want to spend less time on? These time wasters should eliminate it if possible. Are there some things that one might not need anymore? You should remove these things. We have a limited time here on earth, we should strive to eliminate things that are unnecessary.

Sources:

"Is it not madness and the wildest lunacy to desire so much when you can hold so little? ... [it is folly] to think that it is the amount of money and not the state of mind that matters!" -Seneca

"For my part, I would choose sickness rather than luxury, for sickness harms only the body, but luxury destroys both body and soul. Luxury induces weakness in the body, cowardice and lack of self-control in the soul; and further it begets injustice and covetousness in others, and in self the failure in one's duty to friends, city and the gods. ... So, then, as being the cause of injustice, luxury and extravagance must be shunned in every way."
- Musonius Rufus

"The more of these things a man deprives himself of, or of other things like them, or even when he is deprived of any of them, the more patiently he endures the loss, just in the same degree he is a better man." - Marcus Aurelius

"It's not the daily increase but the daily decrease. Hack away at the unessential." - Bruce Lee

"Do not hang your house round with tablets and pictures, but decorate it with moderation: for the one of a foreign (unsuitable) kind, and a temporary deception of the eyes; but the other is a natural and indelible, and perpetual ornament of the house"
- Epictetus

Aurelius, M., & Long, G. (2018). The meditations. Mineola, New York.: Dover Publications.

Epictetus. (2004). Enchiridion. Mineola, NY: Dover Publ.

Lee, B., & Little, J. (2015). Striking Thoughts: Bruce Lee's Wisdom for Daily Living. Tuttle Publishing.

Rufus, C. M., Irvine, W. B., & King, C. A. (2011). Musonius Rufus: Lectures & sayings. Lexington, KY: Createspace.

Internalizing the Sage

Other names: Imaging Daemon, Consult with the Sage

Practice:

· Visualization of a sage to assist in virtuous living.

Intent:

· To have a sage or idol helping to direct rational thought.

· To have the daemon / sage keep one in check.

· To allow constant feedback from an ideal figure.

Effect:

· Allows for rational thought and contemplation.

· Aligns one's self with principles.

· Holds the user accountable to their principles.

Example:

The inner Daemon method may be seen as a literal copy of one's future wise self, or an idol or ideal figure one would want as their personal critic. This "daemon" would "sit" on your shoulder and might help direct the you in rational thought or decisions throughout the day. You might reference this daemon - which may be your wiser future self or may be a miniature Marcus Aurelius - about your actions and about other's actions towards yourself. The daemon keeps you in check, it is always watching over your shoulder and criticizing actions and responses to situations. This would hold the you accountable. This might be also be seen as a personification of one's rational self, or reflective part of the mind which possesses the capacity to take a step back, analyze one's own reactions to events, then voluntarily choose to either respond constructively, or not at all, as reason dictates.

The Stoics also used the Stoic sage as a role model. This is very similar to the daemon; this would be called internalizing the sage. The Sage is an ideal, he is the perfectly virtuous, and wise being. In difficult situations, ask yourself: "What would the Sage do?", "How would he act?", "How would he feel?" You might Imagine that he is watching and observing you and you want to be as good as you can during his watch.

Sources:

"We need to set our affections on some good man and keep him constantly before our eyes, so that we may live as if he were watching us and do everything as if he saw what we were doing." - Seneca

"When you wish to delight yourself, think of the virtues of

those who live with you; for instance, the activity of one, the modesty of another, the liberality of a third, and some other good quality of a fourth. For nothing delights so much as the examples of the virtues when they are exhibited in the morals of those who live with us and present themselves in abundance, as far as is possible. Hence we must keep them before us." - Marcus Aurelius

"If anything is possible for man, and peculiar to him, think that this can be attained by thee." - Marcus Aurelius

"When you are going to confer with anyone, and especially with one who seems your superior, represent to yourself how Socrates or Zeno would behave in such a case, and you will not be at a loss to meet properly whatever may occur." - Epictetus

"Someone may wonder why I go about in private, giving advice and busying myself with the concerns of others, but do not venture to come forward in public and advise the state. I will tell you the reason of this. You have often heard me speak of an oracle or sign which comes to me, and is the divinity which Meletus ridicules in the indictment. This sign I have had ever since I was a child. The sign is a voice which comes to me and always forbids me to do something which I am going to do, but never commands me to do anything, and this is what stands in the way of my being a politician." - Socrates

Aurelius, M., & Long, G. (2018). The meditations. Mineola, New York.: Dover Publications.

Epictetus. (2004). Enchiridion. Mineola, NY: Dover Publ.

Plato, Xenophon, & Denyer, N. (2019). The Apology of Socrates. Cambridge: Cambridge University press.

Seneca, L. A., & Campbell, R. (2014). Letters from a Stoic Epistulae morales ad Lucilium. London: Penguin Classics, an imprint of Penguin Books.

Objective Reframing

Practice:

· Take something you associate a certain emotion and meaning with; reframe it objectively: see it for what it is. Understand the impression vs. reality.

Intent:

· To realize the distinction between the impression of a thing and the reality.

Effect:

· To look at things in a very literal sense.
· To weigh our impression.

Example:

You might want to look at some things and situations objectively. A very intimate activity such as sex is just the friction of a membrane and the ejection of mucus. The beauty of music and emotion attached to it is nothing more than vibrations in the air. The first bike that you ever owned has been destroyed; it reality it is just a replaceable mode of transportation.

Sources:

"And in sexual intercourse that it is no more than the friction of a membrane and a spurt of mucus ejected." - Marcus Aurelius

"Everything we hear is an opinion, not a fact. Everything we see is a perspective, not the truth." - Marcus Aurelius

"You have power over your mind – not outside events. Realize this, and you will find strength." - Marcus Aurelius

Aurelius, M., & Long, G. (2018). The meditations. Mineola, New York.: Dover Publications.

Speak Without Judging

Practice:

· Speak in honesty and without judgment in speech. One should remove opinion and hyperbole from both mental and verbal observations. This might be used in response to others.

Intent:

· Prevent preconceived perceptions from affecting one's perspective and speech.

Effect:

· Viewing the world as objectively as possible.
· Reducing the impact of our initial impressions.

Example:

You see someone who you think has a "bad" haircut. Do not think of them as having a bad haircut but only that they have a certain style or appearance. The hairstyle might initially be seen by someone as "bad." In reality the hairstyle is alopecia from having cancer and we misjudged.

Sources:

"Someone bathes in haste; don't say he bathes badly, but in haste. Someone drinks a lot of wine; don't say he drinks badly, but a lot. Until you know their reasons, how do you know that their actions are vicious? This will save you from perceiving one thing clearly, but then assenting to something different." – Epictetus

"Generally, we're all doing the best we can... We are not privy to the stories behind people's actions, so we should be patient with others and suspend our judgment of them, recognizing the limits of our understanding." – Epictetus

Epictetus. (2004). Enchiridion. Mineola, NY: Dover Publ.

Open Observation Walk

Other Names: Walking Meditation

Practice:

· Take a walk with intense focus on the environment.

Intent:

· Enhance mindfulness.

Effect:

· Greater situational awareness.

· Disassociation from lingering attachments.

Example:

This is a technique for increasing mindfulness. An open observation walk focuses on one's environment. This can take place in any location. While walking listen to your footsteps. Observe the world without analysis while walking. Experience your senses without focus on meaning or judgment. Let the sensations wash over you - smells, and sights, and sounds.

Sources:

"We should take wandering outdoor walks, so that the mind might be nourished and refreshed by the open air and deep breathing." – Seneca

Seneca, L. A., & Campbell, R. (2014). Letters from a Stoic - Epistulae morales ad Lucilium. London: Penguin Classics, an imprint of Penguin Books

Use of Self-Deprecating Humor

Practice:

· Use of humor when a person misjudges one's character. this may be used in response to others.

Intent:

· Not allow other's impressions to harm one's self.

Effect:

· Effectively combat another's misjudgments.
· Express humility.

Example:

Someone called you "stupid" because you tripped on a sidewalk. You might state how they must not know you because they would realize you are have fallen for less.

Self-deprecation is a gentle way of showing high self-esteem without losing your sense of humor. With every insult, you appear stronger. Your very willingness to accept attacks and output humor might guide them on how far off they are.

Sources:

"If you learn that someone is speaking ill of you, don't try to defend yourself against the rumours; respond instead with, 'Yes, and he doesn't know the half of it, because he could have said more." - Epictetus

"If anyone tells you that a certain person speaks ill of you, do not make excuses about what is said of you but answer, "He was ignorant of my other faults, else he would not have mentioned these alone.""- Epictetus

"I have to die. If it is now, well then I die now; if later, then now I will take my lunch, since the hour for lunch has arrived – and dying I will tend to later." - Epictetus
"It is more fitting for a man to laugh at life than to lament over it." -Seneca

"If you have an earnest desire of attaining to philosophy, prepare yourself from the very first to be laughed at, to be sneered by the multitude, to hear them say, 'He is returned to us a philosopher all at once' … For remember that, if you adhere to the same point, those very persons who at first ridiculed will afterwards admire you. But if you are conquered by them, you will incur a double ridicule."
- Seneca

"No one is laughable who laughs at himself." – Seneca

Epictetus, & Lebell, S. (1995). The art of living: The classical manual on virtue, happiness, and effectiveness. New York: HarperOne.

Epictetus. (2004). Enchiridion. Mineola, NY: Dover Publ.

Seneca, L. A., & Campbell, R. (2014). Letters from a Stoic – Epistulae morales ad Lucilium. London: Penguin Classics, an imprint of Penguin Books.

Stoic Test Strategy

Practice:

· Use a difficult situation as a challenge to exercise virtue.

Intent:

· A greater expression of virtue.

Effect:

· Reframing of difficult situations into challenges.

Example:

When things happen, you can use the situation to exercise virtue. You might ask yourself: "What is my best response here?", and "How could I apply reason and virtue here and now?"

For example: your car breaks down in the middle of the road. You want to say to yourself "I can use this situation to practice my virtue." Instead of getting angry you might ask yourself what your best response would be to this situation in a reasonable and virtuous way?" One answer may be to say that it is unreasonable to get angry. Another answer might be that you should outline things you could do now that are within your control, such as change the tire, or call a friend

Removal of Impressions

Practice:

· The practice of purposefully removing things such as social media from one's life.

Intent:

· Develop healthy ideas of the reality of the world.
· Detach ourselves from unnecessary impressions.
· More time available in the day.

Effect:

· Things such as social media impact how we think on a day to day basis without us realizing it. This act will help up live a better life.

Example:

A unique problem to the modern era is social media. Social media can influence our emotions, and our thoughts. Many platforms are made in such a way to keep people on as long as possible and influence them. Seeing the highlights of a person's life without and of the negatives gives us a false impression of reality. This can waste time and emotional energy. While social media is a new challenge to us, it is not too hard to see how the Stoics may have handled this challenge.

Jill is looking through her phone settings and sees her screen time. Jill estimates her screen time to be around one hour. They then she sees it is more like 3.5 hours a day, and mostly at night. She does some math and realize that she wastes around 1300 hours a year. Alarmed she decides to stay away from social media to free herself. She logs out of Facebook and deletes the app from her phone. Jill still thinks searching for videos is useful, so she decides to get an addon for her browser to remove comments from videos, and recommended videos.

A few weeks later Jill reflects on this change and realizes that she is sleeping better at night. She is journaling at night instead of looking at her phone at night. She finds more time in her day and decided to work on a new hobby and exercise more. She finds that her life has become more meaningful from this small change.

Sources:

"In the case of everything attractive or useful or that you are fond of, [you should] remember to say just what sort of thing it is," -Epictetus

"set up...a certain character and pattern for yourself which you will preserve when you are by yourself and when you are with other people," -Epictetus

"No, my son, we were born for something other than this; it is not I who am harmed, it is you, my son, who are causing harm to yourself." — Marcus Aurelius

Epictetus. (2004). *Enchiridion*. Mineola, NY: Dover Publ.

Epictetus, & Lebell, S. (1995). The art of living: The classical manual on virtue, happiness, and effectiveness. New York: HarperOne.

Aurelius, M., & Long, G. (2018). The meditations. Mineola, New York.: Dover Publications.

Scheduling

<u>Practice:</u>

· Create a schedule to orient your life around.

<u>Intent:</u>

· Manage your time in an effective manner.

· Live in the present moment.

<u>Effect:</u>

· We have a certain set of time on this earth, use your time in a efficient way, and waste less time on time wasting things.

<u>Example:</u>

      Much of our time in the day may be wasted inadvertently. There may be many things that someone might want to do in a day, but the stress of not knowing when to start on something may let tasks build up and be forgotten. Having a daily plan helps guide us in our actions. When we have a guide to help us, we can try to adhere and make more efficient use of our day.

Tom decides that he would like to make a schedule for himself. He decides to plan his day. He spits it up by morning midday and evenings. He makes sure to schedule breaks throughout the day as well as time for meditation and reading. At first he has trouble sticking to the schedule. He estimates he only stuck to the schedule 20% of the day. He realizes that this is actually a huge improvement without the schedule and makes it a goal of improving a little bit every day. At the end of the month he realizes that he has become extremely efficient in his daily life and grateful he created a schedule for his life.

Daily Scheduling

> *Schedule for the day you*
> *Balance opportunity, enjoyment, and health.*
> *Ask "does this plan work for me, is it realistic?"*
> *"What time wasters can I eliminate?"*

Schedule Review:

> *How effective was my plan?*
> *How can I improve? (what is causing problems?)*
> *Did it improve my life?*

Scheduling Long Term

> *Set goals for yourself (See: setting goals chapter)*
> *Modify and review goals.*
> *Improve things within your sphere of control.*
> *Keep a routine within your ability.*

Sources:

"At dawn, when you have trouble getting out of bed, tell yourself: "I have to go to work — as a human being. What do I have to complain of, if I'm going to do what I was born for — the things I was brought into the world to do? Or is this what I was created for? To huddle under the blankets and stay warm?" -Marcus Aurelius

"It is not that we have a short time to live, but that we waste a lot of it." - Seneca

"He robs present ills of their power who has perceived their coming beforehand." - Seneca

"At every moment keep a sturdy mind on the task at hand, as a Roman and human being, doing it with strict and simple dignity, affection, freedom, and justice—giving yourself a break from all other considerations. You can do this if you approach each task as if it is your last, giving up every distraction, emotional subversion of reason, and all drama, vanity, and complaint over your fair share."
- Marcus Aurelius

"If you want to improve, be content to be thought foolish and stupid with regard to external things. Don't wish to be

thought to know anything; and even if you appear to be somebody important to others, distrust yourself."
– Epictetus

"Nothing great is created suddenly, any more than a bunch of grapes or a fig. If you tell me that you desire a fig, I answer you that there must be time. Let it first blossom, then bear fruit, then ripen" -Epictetus,

Aurelius, M., & Long, G. (2018). The meditations. Mineola, New York.: Dover Publications.

Epictetus. (2004). *Enchiridion.* Mineola, NY: Dover Publ.

Epictetus, & Dobbin, R. F. (2008). Discourses and selected writings. London: Penguin.

Seneca, L. A., & Campbell, R. (2014). Letters from a Stoic – Epistulae morales ad Lucilium. London: Penguin Classics, an imprint of Penguin Books.

Intermediate Practices

Test Your Impressions

Other Names: Review Your Impressions

Practice:

· Test your impression. If it is unhelpful, then choose a different response. No action may be an option.

Intent:

· A retreat from negative impressions of externals.

Effect:

· Correct judgments on the reality of situations.
· A method to correctly defend against improper impressions.
· Obtaining alternative perspectives to a situation such that it undermines certainty in the original impression.

Example:

When something challenges you: first calm down, take a deep breath, and resist the impulse to immediately react. I then ask myself "I'm getting angry... Does this make sense?" then "What exactly happened?" finally ask yourself "Is this in my control?" For the last question if the answer is no, then I will tell myself "it's none of my concern" because it is not within your control.

Sources:

"So make a practice at once of saying to every strong impression: 'An impression is all you are, not the source of the impression.' Then test and assess it with your criteria, but one primarily: ask, 'Is this something that is, or is not, in my control?' And if it's not one of the things that you control, be ready with the reaction, 'Then it's none of my concern.'" - Epictetus

"Remember, it is not enough to be hit or insulted to be harmed, you must believe that you are being harmed. If someone succeeds in provoking you, realize that your mind is complicit in the provocation. Which is why it is essential that we not respond impulsively to impressions; take a moment before reacting, and you will find it easier to maintain control." -Epictetus

Epictetus. (2004). Enchiridion. Mineola, NY: Dover Publ.

Shame Attacking

Other: REBT

Practice:

· Dissolve anxieties of shame and depression.

Intent:

· Develop the skill disputing irrational thoughts and irrational attachment to people's opinion, discerning event from meaning and ultimately transform your sense of identity and philosophy.

Effect:

· Create a potent situation for practicing disputing irrational thoughts and irrational attachment to people's opinion

Example:

A modern approach to attacking shame is through the use of Rational Emotional Behavior Therapy (REBT). This approach is used to help change stressful and self-defeating behaviors, such as shame, aggression, unhealthy eating, and procrastination that might get in the way of your quality of life. According to REBT: our attitudes, our beliefs, our thoughts the way we think about events and the meanings we attach to them, directly affect how we feel and behave. The ABCDE method is a simple way to approach REBT.

A (Activating situation) I tried to do something and failed

B (Irrational Belief I have about A) I must always be successful

C (Consequences of believing B) I feel bad, depressed.

D (Dispute the Irrational Belief in B) where is it written in stone that I must I always be successful?

E. (Effective new thinking to replace B) I would prefer always to be successful but let's be realistic- that isn't very likely, is it- so when I'm not successful I don't need to make myself feel bad.

Some examples of Irrational beliefs (B of ABCDE):

· *I SHOULD never be ashamed*

· *They MUST see it my way*

· *The sun MUST shine tomorrow*

· *I MUST NEVER display weakness*

· *Other people SHOULD behave in the way I want*

· *People who do bad things MUST ALWAYS be punished etc.*

· *People MUST not take me for granted*

· *I CAN'T STAND IT when I feel (embarrassed, bored, sad, lonely, etc.)*

Another method:

You feel like you want to try what a traditional Stoic might do by putting yourself in an awkward disturbing situation (nothing you'd get in serious trouble for) and try to not feeling ashamed by disputing irrational thoughts and assumptions. This might help to desensitization and elimination of faulty feelings.

You go to the busiest street and: yell at the top of your lungs or raise both your hands up in the air as you walk along. You decide another day to dress very unusually and go throughout the day dressed this way. Initially you might feel embarrassed, however you seem to feel less silly and the day goes on.

Sources:

"...Zeno was easily embarrassed, and Crates tried to cure him of this. Crates, desirous of curing this defect in him, gave him a potful of lentil-soup to carry through the Ceramicus; and when he saw that he was ashamed and tried to keep it out of sight, with a blow of his staff he broke the pot spilling the soup on his outfit and embarrassing him more."

"Our philosophy is called Cynic not because we are indifferent to everything, but because we aggressively endure what others, due to being soft or general opinion find unbearable." – Crates

"It's not what happens to you, but how you react to it that matters." - Epictetus

Ellis, A., & Harper, R. A. (1973). A guide to rational living. Hollywood, CA: Wilshire Book.

David, Daniel et al. "50 years of rational-emotive and cognitive behavioral therapy: A systematic review and meta-analysis." Journal of clinical psychology vol. 74,3 (2018): 304-318. doi:10.1002/jclp.22514

The Sedona Method

Practice:

· Whenever encountering yourself in un-Stoic behavior,
  pause and ask yourself:

(Insert the appropriate Stoic behavior for the situation in
the blanks.)

> "Could I _____?" (yes/no)
> "Would I?" (yes/no)
> "When?" (now/not now)

(You might want to repeat the cycle several times.)

Intent:

· *Procheiron.* Effective recollection of the Stoic mindset.

Effect:

· When you genuinely **ask** yourself whether you can do
  something, your mind is forced to go through the
  imagination of the behavior in order to give an answer.
  This is crucial because it resolves the issue of automatic
  propositional answers stored in memory.

Example:

When trying to lose weight I might find myself going to grab ice cream from the freezer. While gathering a bowl and a spoon I stop myself and choose to practice the Sedona method. I would first ask myself "Could I stop myself right now from eating ice cream?" this would seem possible, so I answer "yes". I might then ask myself "would I stop myself from eating ice cream?" this too seems possible; so I answer "yes". I would then finally ask myself "when?" I answer this as "right now".

By imagining it, you are forced to viscerally recall or imagine the actual how-to of the behavior and in turn restores your visceral knowledge of your capacity to do it.

When you genuinely ask would-I, your mind is forced to determine whether the behavior is congruent with your identity and values. If yes, it produces a visceral affirmation that it indeed is.

Now that your mind has no doubt about your ability and integrity of the behavior, and you ask "when" and implying "Would I now?", your mind has to determine the possibility and practicality and appropriateness of the behavior for the current given situation by hypothesizing and imagining. When it's done that and has deemed the behavior practical your mind wants to avoid cognitive dissonance and has no choice but to do it.

Source:

Dwoskin, H. (2003). The Sedona Method. Sedona, AZ: Sedona Press.

Own What You Do

Practice:

· When using reason to decide to perform an action, one should not feel ashamed.

Intent:

· Release oneself from shame of doing a rightful action.

Effect:

· Realize that shame is not rational.
· Understand it is our own perceptions that cause shame.
· Follow through on actions.

Sources:

"When you have decided that a thing ought to be done, and are doing it, never avoid being seen doing it, though the many shall form an unfavorable opinion about it. For if it is not right to do it, avoid doing the thing; but if it is right, why are you afraid of those who shall find fault wrongly?" - Epictetus

"It is not the actions of others which trouble us (for those actions are controlled by their governing part), but rather it is our own judgments. Therefore remove those judgments and resolve to let go of your anger, and it will already be gone. How do you let go? By realizing that such actions are not shameful to you." -Marcus Aurelius

"If you accomplish something good with hard work, the labor passes quickly, but the good endures; if you do something shameful in pursuit of pleasure, the pleasure passes quickly, but the shame endures" - Musonius Rufus

Aurelius, M., & Long, G. (2018). The meditations. Mineola, New York.: Dover Publications.

Epictetus. (2004). Enchiridion. Mineola, NY: Dover Publ.

Rufus, C. M., Irvine, W. B., & King, C. A. (2011). Musonius Rufus: Lectures & sayings. Lexington, KY: Createspace.

Setting & Reviewing: Boundaries, Life Goals, Purpose, Identity

Practice:

· Define one's overarching role / purpose that they wish to attain.

· Create a goal or list of goals to intend on pursuing in order to achieve this role / Purpose.

· Create a list of things you will spend *your time* on and things you will not waste your time on, to achieve your goal.

· Reflect on this list often to make changes as needed.

· Understand and recognize that this plan may change.

Intent:

· To get an overview of your own purpose and duty one's self and others.

· Consciously define and/or reinforce your identity by stating your boundaries.

Effect:

· A clear understanding of one's purpose and identity and place in the world.

· An understanding of how to achieve one's purpose Through setting boundaries.

<u>Example:</u>

Define first what one's main **role / purpose** may be in life. For example, to define yourself living a simple life and to help others. From there define how one would wish to achieve that with **goals**. For example, in order to achieve helping others, I will work as a nurse, and to achieve living in a house I will save up. From here you can list **practices** that you spend your time on that can further your goals such as studying, working as a nurses' aid, and gathering information on how to become a nurse. One can then also look at things that are not productive towards one's goals and identity such as spending time at the bar drinking, spending excess time socializing, playing excessive video games, and anything else not productive to your goals. Then reflect on these roles, goals, and practices often and reassess any changes.

(See next page)

Role / Purpose: to help improve the lives of others

Goals: Work as a nurse/ live simply

Productive Practices to achieve goals

· Studying.

· Working as a nurses' aid.

· Gathering information on how to become a nurse.

Non-productive Practices to achieve goals

· Spending time at the bar drinking.

· Spending excess time socializing.

· Playing excessive video games.

<u>Sources:</u>

"It is not that we have a short time to live, but that we

waste a lot of it. Life is long enough, and a sufficiently generous amount has been given to us for the highest achievements if it were all well invested… So it is: we are not given a short life but we make it short, and we are not ill-supplied but wasteful of it… Life is long if you know how to use it." - Seneca

Seneca, L. A., & Campbell, R. (2014). Letters from a Stoic – Epistulae morales ad Lucilium. London: Penguin Classics, an imprint of Penguin Books.

Problem Focused Meditation

<u>Practice:</u>

· To meditate on one well-defined problem in attempt to solve it or gain new insight.

<u>Intent:</u>

· To focus your attention on one issue and to think deeply on that issue in a structured format
· Resist distractions from solving the problem

<u>Effect:</u>

· New insight or solution for the problem

<u>Example:</u>

Like any other form of meditation, this requires practice. Initially you may find yourself getting distracted easily, but with focused effort this can be done. Find first a location where you might want to practice this meditation. A distraction free environment for maximal focus is recommended, however walking or exercise while doing this practice may also be done. Choose one of these as a location and relax. In any meditation, your attention will wander, but if you persist to focusing on the problem at hand, you will be able to focus on the problem. Define a word that you will use when you find yourself being distracted such as "distraction", when you find yourself drifting and being distracted say "distraction" to reorient yourself; this is a good practice to have for any meditation practice. Next, with specificity and detail, define the problem that you are having. As you meditate define the variables of the problem, things that might attribute to it, and things that do not involve the problem. When these variables are laid out ask yourself "What is the next thing I should do now that I have outlined these variables?" You can then list possible variables that apply and do not apply. If you get stuck and cannot find a solution, while meditating, reframe yourself; look to someone you admire and ask how they might solve the situation.

Tina finds herself struggling in school. She has tried multiple things to try to improve her grades but has not been able to find a solution. She tries Problem Focused Meditation after learning about it. She finds herself easily distracted in general, so she finds a quiet place to meditate. She defines the word "distraction" to remind herself when she becomes distracted. After some time, she narrows her problem from "Struggling in school" to unable to pay attention in school. She thinks of things that happen when she is in school that might distract her such as her phone use, not sleeping much the night before, drinking, and cramming. She comes to realize that she is tired during school and too distracted. Her previous solution of cramming for exams was not a solution to her fundamental issues, but a way to cope with them. She decides to ask herself what Epictetus would do in her situation. She decides to start a regular, and early sleep schedule so that she will be awake for school the next day. She also decides to leave her phone in her car during the day to prevent herself from being distracted. She also plans a long term study schedule to prevent herself from cramming. She finds weeks later that she is much more successful in school.

Sources:

"The first rule is to keep an untroubled spirit. The second is to look things in the face and know them for what they are." - Marcus Aurelius

If you are distressed by anything external, the pain is not due to the thing itself, but to your estimate of it; and this you have the power to revoke at any moment.. - Marcus Aurelius

"This is the mark of perfection of character—to spend each day as if it were your last, without frenzy, laziness, or any pretending." – Marcus Aurelius

Aurelius, M., & Long, G. (2018). The meditations. Mineola, New York.: Dover Publications.

Advanced Practices

Socratic Dialogue

Practice:

· Intended as a group activity. Socratic dialogue is an argument using the question-and-answer method employed by Socrates.

Intent:

· This allows better rhetoric for the questioner and the answerer

· Allows for a better understanding of propositions.

Effect:

· Train a questioner's ability to question.

· Aids the answerer in discovering their own opinions/biases toward certain statements.

· Allows the answerer to better defend their arguments.

· Aids in allowing the answerer to find faults in their own arguments.

Example:

First pick a proposition. Say, "Is committing adultery wrong?" or "what is the nature of the good?" The questioner is trying to ask questions to derive a contradiction from the answer offered. This is done by asking precise questions-asked without preparation and "off the cuff." This will continue to be done until answers fall flat.

Proposition: What is piety?

Answer: Piety is worshipping the gods.

Q1: Is worshipping the gods done to temper their wrath?

A1: Yes

Q2: Is worshipping done in hopes of attaining something akin to bribery?

A2: Yes.

Q3: Is bribing good?

A3: No.

Q4: Then it is not good to bribe the gods.

A4: panu ge (this is a Plato joke, supply 'yes')

Q5: Piety is not a bad thing.

A5: Not at all.

Q6: Bribery is bad.

A6: yes.

Sources:

"The mind is not a vessel to be filled, but a fire to be kindled." – Plutarch

Plato, Tredennick, H., & Tarrant, H. (1954). The last days of Socrates: Euthyphro, the apology, Crito, Phaedo. London: Penguin Books.

Plutarch, & Babbit, F. C. (1957). Plutarch Moralia. London: Heinemann.

Debate / Discourse

Practice:

· This would be a group activity. Two people discuss the pros and cons of a proposition and each person takes a different side of the argument.

Intent:

· Allows for both persons to discover their own opinions/biases toward certain arguments.

· Allows members to better defend their arguments.

· Aids in allowing the members to find faults in their own arguments.

Effect:

· This allows better rhetoric for the questioner and the answerer.

· Allows for a better understanding of propositions.

Example:

The topic for our debate is *(the proposition)*. Each member defines their terms and the key or important words in the topic. One member makes their argument. The other member makes their argument. The first member will then make a rebuttal towards the other. Vice versa.

Sources:

"If you seek Truth, you will not seek to gain a victory by every possible means; and when you have found Truth, you need not fear being defeated." -Epictetus

Epictetus, & Dobbin, R. F. (2008). Discourses and selected writings. London: Penguin.

Stripping Technique

Practice:

· Treat a situation like an onion, consider the core issues and remove the other unimportant layers we add; this way we can act accordingly to a focused approach.

Intent:

· To derive clarity of the situation.

Effect:

· To understand the core principles of a situation.
· To remove excess thought and feeling that may inhibit us from reaching clarity.

Example:

Break down a situation and remove one's biases on it. What are the core issues to this situation? What value does this situation bring to everyone? What type of qualities does this situation require?

There are many things that we might say brings meaning in our lives or our purpose. Using the stripping method to this question we might say the core of this question is to find something fulfilling and meaningful to work towards. We can do this through stripping issues such as money, people perceptions, and acknowledging our own biases.

(See bias pg.)

Sources:

"It is better by assenting to truth to conquer opinion, than by assenting to opinion to be conquered by truth." – Epictetus

Epictetus. (2004). Enchiridion. Mineola, NY: Dover Publ.

Laconic Dialogue

Practice:

· This may be used in response to others. Laconic dialogue refers to the iconic speech of the Laconians. They used short and concise sentences but with meaning and in simple language. One might want to speak plainly and clearly and not ramble on just to hear one's self speak.

Intent:

· Have meaning behind your words without over flowery sentences.

Effect:

· Simple clear and concise message
· Convey a message effectively

Example:

One might make the statement: High quality learning environments are needed and a necessary precondition for facilitation and enhancement of the ongoing learning process. This could also be said as: Children need good schools if they are to learn properly.

Both of the above messages are conveying the

same idea, however one is much more concise and clear. The intention of the first sentence may be to sound intelligent. However, it may come off as pompous, and arrogant. The Second sentence is used to convey a message in as simple terms as possible.

It might be a good idea to listen more in a conversation with another and speak with meaningful and objective sentences. Epictetus said we should only speak if necessary and not about common-place stuff. Observe yourself and others in conversations. Do you see how everyone is trying to connect what is being said with themselves?

Sources:

"[To run a successful kingdom] If he concede to his friends their just share of frank speech, and, so far as lies in his power, do not suffer any of his subjects to be wronged." - Theopompus

"Well, you could try being simpler, gentler. Even now." - Marcus Aurelius

"When the aim is to make a man learn and not merely to make him wish to learn, we must have recourse to the low-toned words of conversation. They enter more easily, and stick in the memory; for we do not need many words, but, rather, effective words." - Seneca

"First learn the meaning of what you say, and then speak."
- Epictetus

"Above all don't gossip about people, praising, blaming or
comparing them." -Epictetus

"In your conversation, don't dwell at excessive length on
your own deeds or adventures. Just because you enjoy
recounting your exploits doesn't mean that others derive
the same pleasure from hearing about them." - Epictetus

"Attempt on every occasion to provide for nothing so
much as that which is safe: for silence is safer than
speaking, And omit speaking whatever is without sense
and reason." - Epictetus

Aurelius, M., & Long, G. (2018). The meditations. Mineola, New
York.: Dover Publications.

Epictetus. (2004). Enchiridion. Mineola, NY: Dover Publ.

Plutarch, Langhorne, J., & Langhorne, W. (1910). The complete
works of Plutarch. New York: Crowell.

Seneca, L. A., & Campbell, R. (2014). Letters from a Stoic
Epistulae morales ad Lucilium. London: Penguin Classics, an
imprint of Penguin Books.

Lectio Divina

<u>Practice:</u>
· Lectio Divina is a way to meditate on passages. It involves intensive reading, meditation, and contemplation on a passage. A technique based in Christianity but may be applied to Stoic teaching. It seeks to derive a deep understanding of writing.

<u>Intent:</u>
· Way of becoming personally immersed in the Stoic readings very personally to have a deeper understanding of its meaning.

<u>Effect:</u>
· Structured order to the reading of passages.
· Deeper understanding of the passages.

<u>Example:</u>
· Read; meditate; contemplation of the passage:
· First a passage of scripture is read with main points noted;
· Then it is re-read and its core meaning is reflected upon;
· Finally it is re read and reflected on in its entirety.

To do this exercise try to allow 30 minutes to read, reflect, and reflect. Your first reading is an opportunity to get to know the passage. You decide to read *On Man & Nature* and start with reading "ALMA NATURA." You are keenly aware of any words or phrases that seem to stick out during this first reading. The second reading of the same passage focuses further on the points that were noted previously. During this time you might ask "Why did the author write this?", "Is a deeper meaning to it?", "How the passage relates to reason, and a life of virtue?" and "What is its meaning?" After the final reading, spend around 10 minutes in silent contemplation. Reflection on the passage into your personal life, how it might affect your life. At this point you might want to jot down some main points or ideas you get out of this passage.

Sources:

Benedictus, and Joseph Thomas. Lienhard. The Fathers of the Church: from Clement of Rome to Augustine of Hippo. Eerdmans, 2009.

Keating, Thomas. Open Mind, Open Heart: 20th Anniversary Edition. Continuum, 2019.

Thoreau, H. (1960). Thoreau on man & nature: Thoreau on man & nature: A compilation.

Practice of Silence

Practice:

· Set some days of the week to practice silence or limited speech, limit yourself from music or the distractions of the television.

Intent:

· Cultivate this silence in everyday life.
· Have an appreciation for silence.

Effect:

· To experience silence and restriction from distractions.

Example:

Take a few days this week and do not let loud music or excessive conversation run rampant. Be alone in your thoughts and talk sparingly. Another way is as a general rule when confronted with an uncomfortable pause in the conversation, let the pause be. When reaching for something witty to say - do not.

Sources:

"Enjoy the Silence Let silence be your general rule; or say only what is necessary and in few words. We shall, however, when occasion demands, enter into discourse sparingly, avoiding such common topics as gladiators, horse-races, athletes; and the perpetual talk about food and drink. Above all avoid speaking of persons, either in the way of praise or blame, or comparison."

– Epictetus

"Be silent for the most part, or, if you speak, say only what is necessary and in a few words. Talk, but rarely, if occasion calls you, but do not talk of ordinary things—of gladiators or horses races or athletes or of meats or drinks—these are topics that arise everywhere " - Epictetus

"Be silent as to services you have rendered, but speak of favors you have received."

- Epictetus

"We have two ears and one mouth, therefore we should listen twice as much as we speak."

- Zeno

"Better to slip with the foot than with the tongue" – Zeno

Epictetus. (2004). Enchiridion. Mineola, NY: Dover Publ.

Goodman, M., Barton, J., & Muddiman, J. (2013). The Apocrypha. Oxford: Oxford University Press.

Deliberate Attachment Rupture

Practice:

· Take an object and become attached with it to the best of your ability over a time period. At the end of this time period destroy / lose / get rid of the object.

· At this point one should become aware of one's attachments and acknowledge the meaning of the object compared to our attachments.

Intent:

· Learn to detach from objects.

· Detaching from objects in a controlled and planned environment may allow one to detach from more difficult objects later.

Effect:

· Become aware of your attachment. Meaning vs thing.

Example:

The classic example is to grow an attachment to one's favorite mug over a period of two weeks. During this time, one's attachment grows towards the mug. At the end of the time period they might destroy the mug. This is to become aware of your attachments to the mug. And to learn to detach from the mug.

Sources:

"Do not seek for things to happen the way you want them to; rather, wish that what happens to happen the way it happens: then you will be happy." - Epictetus

"In the case of particular things that delight you, or benefit you, or to which you have grown attached, remind yourself of what they are. Start with things of little value. If it is china you like, for instance, say, 'I am fond of a piece of china.' When it breaks, then you won't be as disconcerted. When giving your wife or child a kiss, repeat to yourself, 'I am kissing a mortal.' Then you won't be so distraught if they are taken from you." - Epictetus

"This is what you should practice from morning to evening. Begin with the smallest and most fragile things, a pot, or a cup, and then pass on to a tunic, a dog, a horse, a scrap of land; and from there, pass on to yourself, to your body, and the parts of your body, and to your children, your wife, your brothers. Look around you in every direction, and cast these things far away from you. Purify your judgements so that nothing that is not your own may remain attached to you, or become part of yourself, or give you pain when it comes to be torn away from you. And say while you're training yourself day after day, as you are here, not that you're acting as a philosopher (for you must concede that it would be pretentious to lay claim to that title), but that you're a slave on the way to emancipation. For that is true freedom." - Epictetus

Epictetus. (2004). Enchiridion. Mineola, NY: Dover Publ.

Epictetus, & Dobbin, R. F. (2008). Discourses and selected writings. London: Penguin.

Contemplative Meditation

Practice:

· Contemplative meditation is purposeful observation of a specific idea, question, or situation with the goal of receiving insight from inner wisdom.

Intent:

· Obtain answers to specific questions.

Effect:

· Assistance in life decisions.
· Assistance with habits of thought & behavior.

Example:

You might close your eyes, taking a few slow and focused breaths, focusing on the question you have, asking yourself for insight and inner wisdom while sitting in silence. You might also imagine talking to a Stoic such as Marcus Aurelius and explain to him your situation and your question. Define things that are not inside of your control, and the things that are in your control. Then ask Marcus what he would do in this situation. This is an active meditation for inner insight.

Practicing Indifference to Music

Practice:

· Listen to emotion stirring music without incurring emotion.

Intent:

· Maintenance of reason above emotion.

Effect:

· Practice of recognizing emotional state.
· Practice detaching from emotional state.

Example:

You decide that you might have difficulties in retaining Stoic principles under the duress of an emotional state. You decide to try to listen to *Tannhäuser Overture* by *Richard Wagner* and recognize that emotions are okay, however in reality music is just the vibration in the air. This helps you practice detachment from an emotional state. This may also be done with a sad movie or other media.

Retreat into the Self

Other names: Inner Citadel

Practice:

· The Inner Citadel is the fortress within us that nothing from the outside can perturb. This might be especially effective to imagine a castle quite literally in one's mind.

Intent:

· A retreat from negative impressions of externals.

Effect:

· Correct judgments on the reality of situations.
· A method to correctly defend against improper impressions.

Example:

The concept of the Inner Citadel is to form a fortress around your true self, your guiding principles, so that externals cannot produce a discourse without your approval or reason. One might quite literally imagine a castle surrounding them.

· *First is the outside event, which you do not have control over ("My wallet was lost").*

· *Then your mind creates a discourse about this*
  representation ("this is bad").
· *Then we reframe our discourse as objective*
  ("my wallet is lost that is all").
· *Then we choose to agree or disagree with the discourse,*
  which imprints the discourse in our mind and creates it as
  an internal truth (this is not a serious matter).

There are three walls of defense in our citadel here: the discourse, the reframe, and the choice. The citadel is our guide of which we only allow discourse to which we choose to enter our castle (minds) as true.

Sources:

"People seek retreats for themselves in the countryside by the seashore, in the hills, and you too have made it your habit to long for that above all else. But this is altogether unphilosophical, when it is possible for you to retreat into yourself whenever you please; for nowhere can one retreat into greater peace or freedom from care than within one's own soul, especially when a person has such things within him that he merely has to look at them to recover from that moment perfect ease of mind (and by ease of mind I mean nothing other than having one's mind in good order). So constantly grant yourself this retreat and so renew yourself; but keep within you concise and basic precepts that will be enough, at first encounter, to cleanse you from all distress and to send you back without discontent to the life to which you will return." -Marcus Aurelius

Aurelius, M., & Long, G. (2018). The meditations. Mineola, New York.: Dover Publications.

Hadot, P. (2001). The inner citadel: The "Meditations" of Marcus Aurelius. Cambridge, MA.: Harvard U.P.

Koan Questioning

Practice:

· Pose a question to yourself or others that creates a contradiction in your own/their philosophical framework.

Intent:

· Develop a better understanding of your own philosophy and be able to better defend it.
· Change your philosophy if within reason.

Effect:

· This practice lets you have a deeper understanding of your own values.
· Believing a philosophy is a passive exercise, challenging with Koan allows you to develop a stronger and well adjusted philosophical framework.

Example:

This practice, or similar, was believed to have been done at the ancient Stoic's Stoa in Athens. Questions were posed – usually by a teacher - in order to contradict core philosophies of the learners. In particular, the Cynics would pose riddles to challenge younger student's philosophies, and this was may have been where the Stoics picked this up (See Crates and Zeno). There is little information of what is known about the actual line of questioning that Stoics and Cynics might have used. In the Eastern Zen philosophy, Koan questioning was sometimes practiced. A good resource for Koan might be Blue Cliff Record or Zen Koans by Kubose. While not Specifically Stoic, this line of questioning can be applied to the Stoic philosophy in a meaningful way. This may be better done with a group.

Example from Zen:

When asked why he practiced Zen, the student said, "Because I intend to become a Buddha." His teacher picked up a brick and started polishing it. The student asked, "What are you doing?" The teacher replied, "I am trying to make a mirror." The student responded: "How can you make a mirror by polishing a brick?" The teacher replied: "How can you become Buddha by doing zazen? If you understand sitting Zen, you will know that Zen is not about sitting or lying down. If you want to learn sitting Buddha, know that sitting Buddha is without any fixed form. Do not use discrimination in the non-abiding dharma. If you practice sitting as Buddha, you must kill Buddha. If you are attached to the sitting form, you are not yet mastering the essential principle."

Example of possible Stoic questions:

"Does a dog have Stoic nature or not?"

"What is Stoicism?" — "Understanding fate"

"Are sentient beings are inverted. They lose themselves and follow after things."

"What is the essence of being?" — "Mind only"

"What should we do about the world" — "What is the World?"

<u>Sources:</u>

"Koan after koan explores the theme of nonduality. Hakuin's well-known koan, "Two hands clap and there is a sound, what is the sound of one hand?" is clearly about two and one. The koan asks, you know what duality is, now what is nonduality? In "What is your original face before your mother and father were born?" the phrase "father and mother" alludes to duality. This is obvious to someone versed in the Chinese tradition, where so much philosophical thought is presented in the imagery of paired opposites. The phrase "your original face" alludes to the original nonduality."

Hori, Victor Sogen (2000). Koan and Kensho in the Rinzai Zen
    Curriculum

Thomas Cleary (2005) Blue Cliff Record

Gyomay M. Kubose (1973) Zen Koans

Maxims

Maxims of Introspection

"Fate permitting." - Marcus Aurelius

"You have power over your mind, not outside events."
- Marcus Aurelius

"Take care not to make your pain greater by your complaints."- Anon.

"Some things are within your power, and some are not."
-Epictetus

"Misfortune nobly born is good fortune."
-Marcus Aurelius

"It is within my power to derive benefit from every experience."- Epictetus

"Some things are in my power, and some things are not in my power." - Epictetus

"Fearing death is like fearing gossip." - Seneca

"Who has the most? He who desires the least." - Anon.

"What we bear is not so important as how we bear it." - Anon

"Calamity is an opportunity for courage." - Anon.

"Only by exhibiting actions in harmony with the sound words which he has received will anyone be helped by philosophy." - Rufus

"Some things are up to us and some things are not up to us." - Epictetus

"Whatever this is that I am, it is a little flesh and breath, and the ruling part." - Marcus Aurelius

"Prove your words with things." - Seneca

"Rehearse death. To say this is to tell a person to rehearse his freedom. A person who has learned how to die has unlearned how to be a slave." - Seneca

"Begin at once to live, and count each separate day as a separate life."- Seneca.

"If you are distressed by anything external, the pain is not due to the thing itself, but to your estimate of it; and this you have the power to revoke at any moment."
- Marcus Aurelius

"He has the longest of lives who suffers no time to be lost." - Anon.

"The arts serve life, but wisdom rules it." - Anon.

"The happiness of your life depends upon the quality of your thoughts." - Marcus Aurelius

"Man is disturbed not by things, but by the views he takes of them." – Epictetus

"He is a wise man who does not grieve for the things which he has not, but rejoices for those which he has." - Epictetus.

"Although you are not yet a Socrates, you should live as someone who at least wants to be a Socrates." – Epictetus

"Does the captain of a ship manage it better by not attending?" - Epictetus

"Here and now." -Anon.

"It is my good luck that, although this has happened to me, I can bear it without getting upset, neither crushed by the present nor afraid of the future." - Marcus Aurelius

"Life is neither good or bad, it is the space for both good and bad."- Seneca

"Perform every action as though it were your last."
- Marcus Aurelius

"The willing are led by fate, the reluctant dragged. "
 - Cleanthes

"What would have Socrates or Zeno done in this situation?" - Epictetus

"When you rise in the morning, think of what a precious privilege it is to be alive; to breathe, think, to enjoy, to love."- Marcus Aurelius

"No one is good by accident; virtue must be learned."
- Unknown

"Know thyself." - Socrates

"It's not events that cause us suffering, but our opinion about events." - Unknown

"Let us take in with our mind the worst thing that can possibly happen, if we don't want to be mastered by it."
- Seneca

"No one is a laughing-stock who laughs first at himself."
– Seneca

"Being attached to many things, we are weighed down and dragged along with them." - Epictetus

"Education has no goal more important than bringing our preconception of what is reasonable and unreasonable in alignment with nature." - Epictetus

"Doctors keep their scalpels and other instruments handy, for emergencies. Keep your philosophy ready too, ready to understand heaven and earth." - Marcus Aurelius

"Look back over the past, with its changing empires that rose and fell, and you can foresee the future too."
- Marcus Aurelius

"It never ceases to amaze me: we all love ourselves more than other people, but care more about their opinion than our own." - Marcus Aurelius

"The object of life is not to be on the side of the majority, but to escape finding oneself in the ranks of the insane."
- Marcus Aurelius

"Reject only the undesirable things which you can control." - Epictetus

"Do not feel pride in any achievement not immediately your own." - Epictetus

"Sickness harms the body, not the will. Say this to yourself with regard to everything that happens." - Epictetus

"There is a price paid for peace and tranquility; and nothing is to be had for nothing." - Epictetus

"When you see anyone eminent in honors or power, be careful not to be confused by appearances and to pronounce them happy." - Epictetus

"Let not your laughter be loud, frequent, or abundant."
- Epictetus

"Consider how much more frugal are the poor are, and how much more patient of hardship." - Epictetus

"He who is at peace with himself is at peace with all the gods." - Unknown

"Every man has power to make himself happy."
– Unknown

"If we are anxious about the future, it is because we do not use the present." - Unknown

"The best proof that thy soul is calm is thy ability to continue in thine own company." - Unknown

"Fortune has not such long arms as we think; she seizes on no one who is not clinging to her." – Unknown

"Sickness is a hindrance to the body, but not to the will, unless that yields." - Unknown

"This is education, to learn to wish that things should happen as they do." – Unknown

"Of what use is your reading, if it does not give you peace?" - Unknown

"It is not poverty, but covetousness, that causes sorrow. It is not wealth, but philosophy, that gives security."
 - Unknown

"Fortify thyself in contentment, for this is a fortress which cannot be taken easily." - Unknown

"Do you wish to be useful, or to be praised?" - Unknown

"Money is the fool's master, but the wise man's servant."
- Unknown

"Prosperity gives friends; adversity proves them."
- Unknown

"Only the educated are free." - Unknown

"Do not fear that you have wasted your study if you have taught yourself." - Unknown

"The mind is not a vessel to be filled, but a fire to be kindled." - Plutarch

"I don't need a friend who changes when I change and who nods when I nod; my shadow does that much better." - Plutarch

"What we achieve inwardly will change outer reality."
- Plutarch

"Know how to listen, and you will profit even from those who talk badly." - Plutarch

"Adversity is the only balance to weigh friends." - Plutarch

"The whole of life is but a moment of time. It is our duty, therefore to use it, not to misuse it." – Plutarch

"Neither blame or praise yourself." - Plutarch
"In words are seen the state of mind and character and disposition of the speaker." - Plutarch

"A few vices are sufficient to darken many virtues."
- Plutarch

"An unexamined life is not worth living." - Socrates

"One thing only I know, and that is that I know nothing."
- Socrates

"Since every man dies, it is better to die with distinction than to live long." - Musonius Rufus

Maxims of Temperance

"First say to yourself what you would be; and then do what you have to do." - Epictetus

"No great thing is created suddenly, any more than a bunch of grapes or a fig. If you tell me that you desire a fig, I answer you that there must be time. Let it first blossom, then bear fruit, then ripen." - Epictetus

"Allow not sleep to close your wearied eyes until you have reckoned up each daytime deed." - Epictetus

"At daybreak, when reluctant to rise, have this thought ready in your mind: 'I am getting up to do a human being's work.'" - Marcus Aurelius

"Carry out each act as if it were the last of your life, freed from all randomness and passionate deviation from the rule of reason and from pretence and self-love and dissatisfaction with what has been allotted to you."
- Marcus Aurelius

"It is in times of security that the spirit should be preparing itself to deal with difficult times." - Seneca

"What bad habit have you put right today? Which fault did you take a stand against? In what respect are you better?" - Seneca

"Will your fate." - Epictetus

"Restrain desire. Where it is necessary for you to pursue something, do so with discretion and moderation."
— Epictetus

"At a feast, to choose the largest share is suitable to the bodily appetite, but inconsistent with the social spirit. When you eat with another, value the bodies of those things which are set before you, and your courtesy toward your host." - Epictetus

"It is foolish to pray for that good disposition which you are able to give yourself." — Unknown

"A very little can satisfy our necessities, but nothing our desires." - Unknown

"We must conquer our passions, not by strategy, but by main force; not by slight wounds, but by a deadly charge." - Unknown

"A stomach which can wait patiently, and endure rough treatment, is an important condition of liberty."- Unknown

"It is wonderful how much the mind is excited by moving the body." - Unknown

"Employ your time in improving yourself by other men's writings, so that you shall gain easily what others have labored hard for."
- Socrates

"If you accomplish something good with hard work, the labor passes quickly, but the good endures; if you do something shameful in pursuit of pleasure, the pleasure passes quickly, but the shame endures" - Musonius Rufus

"Freedom is not gained by satisfying, but by restraining our desires." - Seneca

"They who do not keep striving to advance fall back; no one finds his progress as he left it."- Seneca

"Virtue does not come until the character is formed, and taught, and developed by continual exercise." - Seneca

"Do nothing inconsiderately or without a purpose." - Seneca

"Control yourself." - Seneca

"Nothing to excess." - Delphi Inscription

"If we were to measure what is good by how much pleasure it brings, nothing would be better than self-control- if we were to measure what is to be avoided by its pain, nothing would be more painful than lack of self-control" - Musonius Rufus

"We will train both soul and body when we accustom ourselves to cold, heat, thirst, hunger, scarcity of food, hardness of bed, abstaining from pleasures, and enduring pains." - Musonius Rufus

"Won't we, therefore, be willing to endure pain in order to gain complete happiness?" - Musonius Rufus

Maxims of Justice

"Objective judgement, now at this very moment."
- Marcus Aurelius

"From first to last review your acts and then reprove yourself for wretched [or cowardly] acts but rejoice in those done well." - Epictetus

"There is usually a lot to learn before any sure-footed moral judgments can be made about other people's actions." - Marcus Aurelius

"What, then, is to be done? To make the best of what is in our power, and take the rest as it naturally happens." - Epictetus

"Everything we hear is an opinion, not a fact. Everything we see is a perspective, not the truth." - Marcus Aurelius

"When you perform any action, remind yourself of what nature the action is." - Epictetus

"Be silent, or speak what is needful, and in few words. You may enter into discourse sometimes, when occasion calls for it. Let it not run into any of the common subjects, and especially not on other people, so as either to blame, or praise, or make comparisons." - Epictetus

"If anyone tells you that a certain person speaks ill of you, do not make excuses about what is said of you. Answer: "They were ignorant of my other faults; else they would not have mentioned these alone." – Epictetus

"The philosopher looks inwards for all help or harm." – Epictetus

"Whatever rules you have adopted, abide by them as laws." - Epictetus

"Liberty is not to be had for free; if she be worth this much to us, all things else will have little value."
- Unknown

"Be like a headland, standing firm against the waves that beat against it continually, and calming the raging sea."
- Unknown

"Let us inflict punishment without anger, and because it is useful, not because revenge is sweet." - Unknown

"If he be your friend, he has done what was not intended; if he be your enemy, what might have been foreseen."
- Unknown|

"Let me be good-natured with my friends, and mild and easy with my enemies." - Unknown

"The wise man will pardon much, and save many souls because they are capable of being healed." - Unknown

"Better leave crime unpunished than condemn the innocent." - Unknown

"He is best and purest who pardons others as if he sinned himself daily, but avoids sinning as if he never pardoned." – Unknown

"No one is owner of another's will." - Unknown

"Peace with all mankind, but war with vice." - Unknown

"From Diognetus I learned to endure freedom of speech." - Unknown

"Better die than live ill." - Unknown

"An imbalance between rich and poor is the oldest and most fatal ailment of all republics." -Plutarch

"The poor go to war, to fight and die for the delights, riches, and superfluities of others." - Plutarch

"It is certainly desirable to be well descended, but the glory belongs to our ancestors." - Plutarch

"To be ignorant of the lives of the most celebrated men of antiquity is to continue in a state of childhood all our days." - Plutarch

"Silence at the proper season is wisdom, and better than any speech." -Plutarch

"It is a thing of no great difficulty to raise objections against another man's oration, it is a very easy matter; but to produce a better in it's place is a work extremely troublesome." - Plutarch

"It is part of a good man to do great and noble deeds, though he risk everything." - Plutarch

"The fact is that men who know nothing of decency in their own lives are only too ready to launch foul slanders against their betters and to offer them up as victims to the evil deity of popular envy." - Plutarch

"If a man is proud of his wealth, he should not be praised until it is known how he employs it." -Socrates

"One who is injured ought not to return the injury, for on no account can it be right to do an injustice; and it is not right to return an injury, or to do evil to any man, however much we have suffered from him." -Socrates

"It is not living that matters, but living rightly." - Socrates

"We begin to lose our hesitation to do immoral things when we lose our hesitation to speak of them."
- Musonius Rufus

"To accept injury without a spirit of savage resentment-to show ourselves merciful toward those who wrong us-being a source of good hope to them-is characteristic of a benevolent and civilized way of life." - Musonius Rufus

Maxims of Benevolence

"Waste no more time arguing what a good man should be. Be one." - Marcus Aurelius

"Good character outshines all possessions." - Seneca

"When one man's bad character reveals fury unfurled, remember that all types must exist in this world."
 - Marcus Aurelius

"If evil be spoken of you and it be true, correct yourself, if it be a lie, laugh at it." - Epictetus

"Be kind to friends." - Anon.

"Happy the man who improves other people not merely when he is in their presence but even when he is in their thoughts." - Seneca

"If you wish to be loved, love. " - Seneca

"Kindness is an irresistible force, so long as it is genuine. "
- Marcus Aurelius

"Men have come into being for one another; so either educate them or put up with them." - Marcus Aurelius

"Rational beings exist for the sake of one another. Thus the leading principle in the constitution of man is concern for the good of others." - Marcus Aurelius

"Say to yourself at daybreak: I shall come across the meddling busy- body, the ungrateful, the overbearing, the treacherous, the envious, and the antisocial. All this has befallen them because they cannot tell good from evil."
- Marcus Aurelius

"We were born for cooperation, like feet, like hands, like eyelids, like the rows of upper and lower teeth. So to work in opposition to one another is against nature."
- Marcus Aurelius

"Associate with people who are likely to improve you. Welcome those who are capable of improving. The process is a mutual one: men learn as they teach." - Seneca

"Let us therefore go all out to make the most of friends, since no one can tell how long we shall have the opportunity." - Seneca

"Accept the things to which fate binds you, and love the people with whom fate brings you together, but do so with all your heart." - Marcus Aurelius

"The best revenge is to be unlike him who performed the injury." - Marcus Aurelius

"If it is not right do not do it; if it is not true do not say it." - Marcus Aurelius

"When another blames you or hates you, or people voice similar criticisms, go to their souls, penetrate inside and see what sort of people they are. You will realize that there is no need to be racked with anxiety that they should hold any particular opinion about you." - Marcus Aurelius

"You are an actor in a drama. Act well the part." – Epictetus

"It is peculiarly human to love even those who do wrong." - Unknown

"It is a part of thine own constitution, as well as of the nature of man, to do philanthropic acts." - Unknown

"Treat men fraternally, because they are endowed with reason." - Unknown

"Do nothing but what is useful to men." – Unknown

"We should be neither squeamish nor abject in taking favors." - Unknown

"To find fault is easy; to do better may be difficult."
- Plutarch

"Do not speak of your happiness to one less fortunate than yourself." - Plutarch

"For mankind, evil is injustice and cruelty and indifference to a neighbor's trouble, while virtue is brotherly love and goodness and justice and beneficence and concern for the welfare of your neighbor—with" - Musonius Rufus

Affect Heuristic
A mental shortcut used to make decisions quickly by bringing their emotional response into play. They make decisions according to their gut feeling or instinct.

Anchoring
A cognitive bias that describes the human tendency to rely heavily on the first piece of information offered when making decisions.

Availability Heuristic
A mental shortcut that relies on immediate examples or images that comes to a person's mind when evaluating a specific topic, concept, method or decision.

Bounded Rationality
In decision making, it is the idea that people might be limited by the information they have. The cognitive limitations of their mind prevents them from maximizing their options, they seek something "good enough" as a result.

Certainty Effect
When people overweigh outcomes that are considered certain relative to outcomes that are possible.

Choice Overload

A cognitive process in which people have a difficult time making a decision when faced with too many options. Too many choices may also cause people to delay making decisions or avoid them.

Cognitive Dissonance

Occurs when people's beliefs do not match with their behaviors.

Commitment

The tendency to be consistent with what we have already done or said we will do in the past.

Confirmation Bias

The tendency to search for or interpret information in the way that confirms one's preexisting beliefs, leading errors.

Decision Fatigue

A decreased quality of decisions made after a long session of decision making.

Decoy Effect

When there are only two options, people will tend to make decisions according to their personal preferences. When offered another option, they will be more likely to choose the more expensive of the two original options.

Dunning-Kruger Effect

A cognitive bias in which people who are ignorant in a given domain tend to believe they are much more competent than they are.

Time Discounting

The tendency of people to want things now rather than later.

Diversification Bias

People seek more variety when they choose multiple items for future consumption than when they make choices sequentially on an 'in the moment' basis.

Endowment Effect

Once people own something they irrationally overvalue it, regarding of its objective value.

Fear of Missing Out

An anxious feeling that one might fear that other people might be having rewarding experiences that they are missing.

Framing Effect

People mostly avoid risk when a positive frame is presented but seek risks when a negative frame is presented.

Monte Carlo Fallacy

The mistaken belief that, if something happens more frequently than normal during a certain period of time, it will happen less frequently in the future.

Halo Effect

Bias in which our overall impression of a person influences how we feel and think about a persons character.

Herd Behavior

The tendency for individuals to mimic the actions of a larger group. Most people would not necessarily make the same choice if not identified with a group.

Hindsight Bias

The tendency of people believe they could have predicted an outcome that could not possibly have been predicted; this can result in an oversimplification in cause and effect.

In-Group Bias

In-Group Bias is the unfair favoring of someone from one's own group.

Less-Is-Better Effect

Low-value options are valued more highly than high-value options.

Optimism Bias

This causes people to believe that they are at a decreased risk of experiencing a negative event compared to others.

Overconfidence Effect

Overestimation of knowledge and ability to predict.

Over justification Effect

Being rewarded for doing something diminishes intrinsic motivation to perform that action.

Peak-End Rule
Judgement of an experience largely based on how they felt at its peak.

Priming
When exposed to one stimulus, it affects how they respond to another stimulus.

Projection Bias
Overestimation of the degree that other people agree with one's self.

Reciprocity
When someone does something for a person, they naturally want to do something in return for them.

Regret aversion
People anticipate regret if they made a wrong choice, and take this anticipation into consideration when making future decisions.

Representativeness Heuristic
People judge the probability of an event by finding a similar event and assuming that the probabilities will also similar.

Scarcity
The difficulty of acquiring an item increases the value that item has.

Self-Serving Bias
We attribute successes and positive outcomes to our doing, but negative outcomes are attributed to contextual factors outside.

Social proof
Referencing the behavior of others to guide their own behavior.

Sunk Cost Fallacy
Irrationally following through on an activity that is not meeting their expectations time or money that has already been spent.

Dwyer, C.P. (2017). Critical thinking: Conceptual perspectives and practical guidelines. Cambridge, UK: Cambridge University Press; with foreword by former APA President, Dr. Diane F. Halpern.

Dwyer, C. P., Hogan, M. J., & Stewart, I. (2014). An integrated critical thinking framework for the 21st century. Thinking Skills & Creativity

Fabre, J.-M., and Gonzalez, M.. Cognitive Biases. Netherlands, Elsevier Science, 1990.

Forer, B. R. (1949) "The Fallacy of Personal Validation: A classroom Demonstration of Gullibility," Journal of Abnormal Psychology

Kahneman, D. (2011). Thinking fast and slow. Penguin: Great Britain.

Kruger, J. &Dunning, D. (1999). Unskilled and unaware of it: How difficulties in recognizing one's own incompetence lead to inflated self-Assessments. Journal of Personality and Social Psychology

Pohl, Rüdiger F. Cognitive Illusions: A Handbook on Fallacies and Biases in Thinking, Judgement and Memory. United Kingdom, Taylor & Francis, 2012.

Tversky, A. & Kahneman, D. (1974). Judgment under uncertainty: Heuristics and biases. Science

West, R. F., Toplak, M. E., & Stanovich, K. E. (2008). Heuristics and biases as measures of critical thinking: Associations with cognitive ability and thinking dispositions. Journal of Educational Psychology

Stoic Rules

The Three Areas of Epictetus

"There are three areas of study, in which a person who is going to be good and noble must be trained. That concerning desires and aversions, so that he may never fail to get what he desires nor fall into what he would avoid. That concerning the impulse to act and not to act, and, in general, appropriate behavior; so that he may act in an orderly manner and after due consideration, and not carelessly. The third is concerned with freedom from deception and hasty judgement, and, in general, whatever is connected with assent." — *Epictetus*

1.   The Discipline of Assent.

We study and exercise ourselves in the Discipline of Assent that we may keep our *prohairesis* in a state conformable to nature. *Prohairesis* represents the choice involved in giving or withholding assent to impressions.

2.   The Discipline of Desire.

Study and exercise ourselves in the Discipline of Desire and aversions that we may have eagerness of true goods, aversions to true evils, and then not lost in apparent goods and evils.

3.   The Discipline of Action.

We study and exercise ourselves in the Discipline of Action and Inaction that we may fulfill our duties by undertaking actions with justice, self-discipline, courage, and practical wisdom.

The Seven Precepts of Musonius

"If you accomplish something good with hard work, the labor passes quickly, but the good endures; if you do something shameful in pursuit of pleasure, the pleasure passes quickly, but the shame endures."— *Musonius,*

1.   To speak plainly, and true.

Speak truly and with virtue in mind. If what we say is true, and the listener is of a reasonable mind, we do not need to repeat, or embellish. Speak simply and directly. Take note of our emotions when we speak and how we project ourselves. "One begins to lose his hesitation to do unseemly things when one loses his hesitation to speak of them."

2.   To prefer practice to theory alone.

Practice what we learn. Practice is mark of the philosopher who is actively living philosophy as a way of life. It is no good to learn of philosophy without putting it into action. If there is some sort of thing we struggle with, we should surly practice at it. It is good to think of virtue, but if all we do is think of it only it is pointless.

3. To eat no animal-flesh, with moderation and simply.

We should eat for health, with self-control, and according to our nature. He states to not eat of animals here, but only that which is produced by them. It could be debated that eating of animals is of our nature. Musonius also states that the foundation of moderation begins with eating. Perhaps by eating once or twice a day.

4. To dress simply, for protection of the body, and without vanity.

To dress minimally for function and modesty; not to show off or be immodest. Why is it that we dress in certain ways, is it for function and in what manner? Moderation should be applied to dress.

5. To cut not the beard, and the hair only to remove what is useless.

Leave the beard, nature's symbol of the male, as it is formed by Nature. Only cut the other hair as necessity and utility may demand, not for fashion nor to appear beautiful in the eyes of others. Hair is not an issue, unless like feathers to a bird, it becomes in excess that they can no longer function. Other Stoic philosophers too made similar comments. Epictetus stated that the beard is placed by nature as the symbol of the male, like the rooster's comb, or lion's mane. More extreme Epictetus stated that the beard is a matter of piety, so important he would accept death rather than to go against nature by cutting it. "Come now, Epictetus, shave off your beard," to which Epictetus replied: "If

I am a philosopher, I answer, I will not shave it off." "Then I will have you beheaded," to which Epictetus again replied: "It if will do you any good, behead me."

6. To strengthen the body and soul through cold and heat, thirst and hunger, scarcity of food and hardness of bed, and abstaining from pleasure and enduing pain.

We should practice temperance, and even asceticism so that we might become more wise, more just, more temperate, and more courageous. Epictetus states on this: "I am inclined to pleasure: in order to train myself I will incline beyond measure in the opposite direction. I am disposed to avoid trouble: I will harden and train my impressions to this end, that my will to avoid may hold aloof from everything of this kind." Of the types of training he states there are two types: of the soul and body, and of the soul alone.

Of the Soul and Body:

cold and heat	*thirst and hunger*	*smaller rations*
hard beds	*avoidance of pleasure*	*patience under suffering*

Of The Soul Alone:

build the habit of handling impressions appropriately

have the proofs in mind regarding apparent and real goods and evils

distinguish between apparent and real goods and evils

practice in not avoiding apparent evils

practice in not pursuing apparent goods

practice in avoiding real evils

practice in pursuing real goods.

7.   To use sex only for virtuous purposes, and within the confines of fidelity.

We take it upon ourselves to use our sexual faculties with kindness and virtue. He states that sexual activity is only acceptable within the confines of marriage. Musonius valued the institution of family and the bond with it. He also wrote that people should not be slaves to it.

Some Stoic Rules for Living

1. *Worry what depends on you first then others.*

2. *Love fate, accept it.*

3. *Impose yourself some discomfort every day.*

4. *Learn to be happy with very little.*

5. *Frequently imagine losing things you hold dear.*

6. *Remember that you will die, you are mortal.*

7. *Happiness comes from within, not from external.*

8. *Be quick not to anger.*

9. *All is only present. Past and future are nonexistent.*

10. *Anxiety is worry of the future, and irrational.*

11. *Depression is living in the past, and irrational.*

12. *Living in the present is peace.*

13. *Be tolerant with others.*

14. *Be strict with yourself.*

15. *Do not to show, but to be better.*

16. *Be wise with your wallet.*

17. *Keep a list of persons dear to you, and why.*

18. *Wake up early and sleep early every day.*

19. *If it is not right do not do it.*

20. *If it is not true do not say it.*

21. *Speak simply and directly.*

22. *Create goals but do not be bound to them.*

23. *See things for what they are.*

24. *Know all problems are yours alone.*

25. *Live and practice the four virtues.*

Made in the USA
Middletown, DE
12 November 2021